Cambodia

Ian Brown

Oxfam

First published by Oxfam GB in 2000

© Oxfam GB 2000

ISBN 0 85598 430 9

Available from the following agents:

USA: Stylus Publishing LLC,
  PO Box 605, Herndon, VA 20172-0605, USA
  tel: +1 (0)703 661 1581; fax: + 1(0)703 661 1547;
  email: styluspub@aol.com; website www.styluspub.com

Canada: Fernwood Books Ltd,
  PO Box 9409, Stn. 'A', Halifax, N.S. B3K 5S3, Canada
  tel: +1 (0)902 422 3302; fax: +1 (0)902 422 3179;
  e-mail: fernwood@istar.ca

India: Maya Publishers Pvt Ltd,
  113-B, Shapur Jat, New Delhi-110049, India
  tel: +91 (0)11 649 4850; fax: +91 (0)11 649 1039;
  email: surit@del2.vsnl.net.in

K Krishnamurthy,
  23 Thanikachalan Road, Madras 600017, India
  tel: +91 (0)44 434 4519; fax: +91 (0)44 434 2009;
  email: ksm@md2.vsnl.net.in

South Africa, Zimbabwe, Botswana, Lesotho, Namibia, Swaziland:
  David Philip Publishers,
  PO Box 23408, Claremont 7735, South Africa
  tel: +27 (0)21 64 4136; fax: +27(0)21 64 3358;
  email: dppsales@iafrica.com

Tanzania: Mkuki na Nyota Publishers,
  PO Box 4246, Dar es Salaam, Tanzania
  tel/fax: +255 (0)51 180479, email: mkuki@ud.co.tz

Australia: Bush Books,
  PO Box 1958, Gosford, NSW 2250, Australia
  tel: +61 (0)2 043 233 274; fax: +61 (0)2 092 122 468,
  email: bushbook@ozemail.com.au

Rest of the world: contact Oxfam Publishing,
  274 Banbury Road, Oxford OX2 7DZ, UK.
  tel. +44 (0)1865 311 311; fax +44 (0)1865 313 925;
  email publish@oxfam.org.uk;
  website www.oxfam.org.uk/publications.html

Printed by
  Information Press, Eynsham, Oxford

Published by
  Oxfam GB, 274 Banbury Road, Oxford OX2 7DZ, UK

Series designed by
  Richard Morris, Stonesfield Design.
  This title designed by Richard Morris.
  Typeset in FF Scala and Gill Sans.

Cover designed by
  Rowie Christopher

Oxfam GB is a registered charity, no. 202 918, and is a member of Oxfam International.

Contents

Jim Holmes

Learning to trust

Jim Holmes

▲ *Chhoun Yeath, farmer and mother, at home in Takorm village, Battambang Province*

Chhoun Yeath's story of trust destroyed

Chhoun Yeath is a farmer. She lives with five of her seven children in a small wooden house on stilts in the village of Takorm in Battambang Province, north-west Cambodia. Like most of Cambodia's rural people, her life revolves around the seasonal rice crop, due to be harvested shortly. 'I don't expect a good crop this year,' she says. 'There hasn't been enough rain. The previous three years haven't been good either, because of flooding.' She is worried, too, about repaying a loan to a commercial rice-lender. She has heard that people in the area have been forced to give up their land to settle unpaid debts. However, she is determined not to lose her two-hectare plot.

'Life has been difficult since my husband died in 1995,' Yeath continues. 'He died in his sleep. He may have suffered a heart attack, though I'm still not sure of the cause. It happened so suddenly. I regret not being able to care more for him. He was a good man. He worked hard and didn't drink too much. I trusted him.' Yeath pauses, contemplating her last sentence as though she has said something unusual. She appears to withdraw, staring away into the distance, but she gathers herself and begins speaking again, with less emotion than before.

'My husband and I were married in a ceremony organised by the Khmer Rouge in early 1978. We didn't know each other before the wedding. *Angkar* ['the organisation', denoting the Communist Party of Kampuchea during the Khmer Rouge period] arranged everything for us. We were allowed two days together, and then we were separated. I missed him. We worked in different mobile teams. I was with women, he with men, and we could only rarely see each other. It was sad that we couldn't share anything as husband and wife. Fortunately we both survived the Khmer Rouge period, but we lost family members. My mother died of starvation, though no one told me until after her death. I knew she was ill, but I was refused permission to visit her. When I eventually arrived in my mother's village, she had already been buried. According to Buddhist tradition we should cremate the body, but *Angkar* would not allow that, so she was buried. I still feel angry that I wasn't there to tend to her and grieve for her. The Khmer Rouge destroyed our families. They took away the trust between children and parents, training children to spy on their mothers and fathers. They took away the trust between husband and wife, brother and sister, because survival meant looking after yourself. Even today, people still mistrust each other. It is hard to understand the mind of another person, to know if that person is going to be loyal or not. And without trust, we cannot move forward.'

And trust rebuilt ...

Yeath and her fellow villagers are moving forward. In 1992, they formed a village development committee (VDC) whose role is not only to provide support to the most vulnerable people in Takorm, but also to give villagers the opportunity to work together to solve problems, creating solidarity and mutual trust in place of suspicion. Yeath was elected vice-president of the VDC in 1996 and she plays an active role on the committee. The village now has a rice bank, which lends rice to members at a fraction of the interest levied by commercial lenders – though the reserves are not yet big enough to satisfy all the members' needs – and a cow bank, providing animals for ploughing and transporting goods. For Yeath, the material support is only one benefit of the VDC: 'It also gives us time to sit down and talk to each other about what is happening, and to work together. We have learned that we have no choice but to trust one another, if we are going to improve our lives.'

▼ The soil in Battambang Province is dark and rich: ideal for growing rice, which is Cambodia's main crop

Nic Dunlop

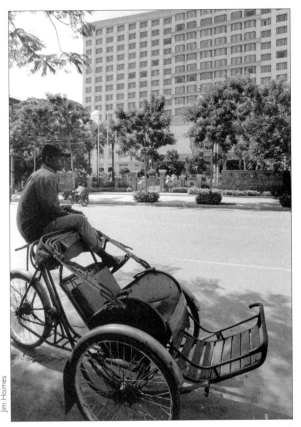

Jim Holmes

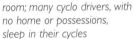

▲ Poverty and wealth: the five-star Cambodiana Hotel charges £140 a night for a room; many cyclo drivers, with no home or possessions, sleep in their cycles

Poverty in Cambodia

This book describes the lives of Yeath and her children and five other Cambodian families, and the ways in which they are facing up to the challenges of a rapidly changing society. They come from different parts of the country: from the plains of the north-west and the highland forests of the north-east, from the banks of the Tonle Sap River and the urban sprawl of Phnom Penh, the capital city. They are rice farmers, fisherpeople, tradespeople, and casual labourers – or combinations of the four. They are from different ethnic groups, speak different languages, and follow different belief systems. What they have in common is that they live in poverty.

According to the United Nations Development Programme, Cambodia is one of the poorest countries in south-east Asia and the world, ranked 140th out of 174 in the UNDP index of human development. But it should not be ranked so low. Although the birth-rate is increasing, there is still enough arable land to feed the whole country and provide the predominantly rural population with a secure livelihood, despite irregular rainfall and occasional flooding and poor soil quality in some areas. Rivers and lakes hold plentiful stocks of fish, and supplies of good-quality timber and other products are to be found in Cambodia's forests. Reserves of precious gemstones and other minerals lie beneath the earth. And yet more than one-third of the total population of 11.4 million – most of them living in rural areas – live below the poverty line, while a conspicuous minority enjoys immense wealth.

Why should there be so many poor people in a country endowed with valuable natural resources? And why should the benefits be restricted to a privileged few? This book will try to answer these questions, examining the causes of poverty and ways in which the poor are challenging those causes. Rebuilding trust at all levels of society is the overarching theme.

Poverty is a complex phenomenon. It seldom has a single cause. More realistically it is a syndrome whereby a number of factors, influences, and circumstances combine to determine who gains and who loses, who is powerful and who is powerless, who is rich and who is poor. But poverty is not inevitable. We do not live in a world determined by fate. Poverty is man-made and, by logical extension, it can be 'unmade'.

The legacy of war

Cambodia is no exception. When the Khmer Rouge were forced to flee an invading Vietnamese army in 1979, they left behind a shattered, traumatised people and an economy on the verge of collapse. At least 1.7 million Cambodians had died from starvation, exhaustion, disease, and execution; half the population was displaced; hundreds of thousands fled into Thailand to escape the onset of famine. Yeath's story of life under the Khmer Rouge hints at some of the pain felt by all Cambodians who survived the Maoist-inspired experiment in social control. Twenty years on, the survivors still bear the psychological scars of the experiment, which achieved nothing but the destruction of the fabric of society. The perpetrators of the genocide have yet to be judged.

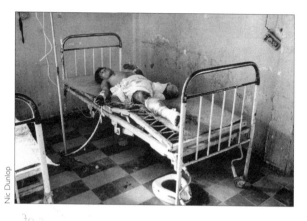

▲ Hospital facilities are grossly inadequate. This landmine casualty died five days after an operation to amputate his remaining leg

War is one of the main causes of poverty in Cambodia. In the early 1970s, US President Richard Nixon, enmeshed in the Vietnam War, secretly extended the theatre of conflict into Cambodia, with the aim of destroying communist bases and supply trails. American bombs killed 150,000 people and destroyed towns, villages, and infrastructure. In 1975 the Khmer Rouge seized power from Lon Nol, the puppet ruler of Cambodia backed by the USA. It took the Khmer Rouge under the leadership of Pol Pot only four years to achieve the virtual annihilation of Cambodian society. Then from 1979 to 1998 they fought a ruthless guerrilla war against successive Cambodian governments, causing widespread displacement of innocent civilians, laying deadly landmines and booby traps to prevent access to arable land, and sabotaging vital economic installations. Once more, people in rural areas bore the brunt of the violence. And they will go on doing so until several million landmines, planted by governments and rebels alike, are safely removed.

Thirty years of conflict and a decade of political and economic isolation, imposed on Cambodia in the 1980s by the USA, China, and western European powers following the Vietnamese invasion in 1979, have prevented real economic development from taking root at all levels of society. In addition, conflict and insecurity have allowed successive Cambodian regimes to justify an extremely high proportion of spending on arms (over 50 per cent of the budget in July 1998) in place of much-needed investment in social services. The shortfall in funds for health care and education has to be made up by contributions from the public. Those who cannot pay are excluded. Consequently tuberculosis and malaria are endemic among the poor; HIV/AIDS is spreading and soon will be endemic; and literacy rates are the lowest in south-east Asia. Women suffer disproportionately high levels of ill health and poor education compared with men. Foreign aid helps to plug some of the holes, but only concerted political will can bring about sustainable improvements to people's lives.

Poverty, politics, and the free-for-all

But what of the supply of natural resources at the disposal of the state? Since the end of the Vietnamese-backed People's Republic of Kampuchea in 1989, Cambodian governments have abandoned State central planning in favour of the free market and private ownership. Large swathes of agricultural land, waterways, and forests, whether previously under State control or not, have been appropriated by the private sector, often with the connivance of political leaders, more interested in quick profit than in protecting the long-term rights of the people, who are subsequently denied access to areas where they traditionally worked. Corruption now reaches the highest echelons of government and the army; some ministers and high-ranking officers are allegedly involved in illegal logging. Collaboration between political, military, and economic elites has meant vast fortunes for the few and growing impoverishment for the many.

The free market has become a free-for-all, where the rule of law does not apply to those who have the means to graft. In the absence of an independent judiciary to offer protection against the excesses of big business, the poor risk getting ever poorer. And they know it. That is why they are working together to protect their livelihoods and 'unmake' their poverty. The VDC in Yeath's village of Takorm is only one of hundreds of village-based organisations that have been set up to give people a fair chance to make a living and escape the pernicious trap of debt and, in doing so, to take more control over their lives; elsewhere, forest dwellers are taking direct action to oppose environmental destruction; Cambodians are forming non-government organisations (NGOs) to defend the poor; and ordinary men and women are taking to the streets to march for peace and to protest against violations of human rights committed by the state.

Our six families are players in this quest for a decent life for themselves and their communities. They are not exceptional, nor are they victims. They face daily hardship, but their stories resound with courage and resilience. They all share the hope that they will live in a society at peace with itself after so many years of violence; and they know that, to achieve their hopes, rebuilding trust among all Cambodians is indispensable.

▼ A logging truck heads towards the sawmills of Battambang town. Cambodia's forests are under severe threat from illegal felling

Jim Holmes

Cambodia today: a world of change

Painting the whole picture

In the minds of Westerners, there are two common – and completely contradictory – images of Cambodia. At one extreme is the romantic notion of a timeless, verdant country of smiling, gentle people, 'an idyllic, antique land unsullied by the brutalities of the modern world', as William Shawcross, writer on Cambodian affairs, described the perception of some foreign diplomats during the 1960s. At the other extreme is a place of unspeakable savagery, epitomised by the film *The Killing Fields*, which portrayed life under the Khmer Rouge in horrific detail: systematic torture, execution, nightmarish scenes of a brutalised population, silently enduring hunger and disease, at the hands of one of the most sadistic regimes of modern times.

Both impressions contain elements of truth: rural Cambodia, although scarred by deep wounds inflicted by the Khmer Rouge, is still very traditional in many ways: a land of the living past; in the cities the imperturbable calm of Buddhist monks, clad in saffron robes, contrasts with the ugliness of violence and crime. But these impressions tell only a part of the story. Cambodian society is undergoing dynamic change, due in large part to a political decision in the late 1980s to transform the economy from a socialist, centrally planned system to a free-market model. Cambodia is more than ever exposed to strong regional winds of change. For those with the means to exploit it, the free market has brought a better standard of living and financial security. For those who had few resources to start with, life has become even more of a struggle to survive. And with economic upheaval have come changes in the social and political order. For rich and poor, men and women, Cambodia today is very different from Cambodia a decade ago.

▼ *The traditions of the past are being challenged by the new global economic order.*

Jim Holmes

The past shapes the present

Cambodia today is shaped by her past. Once a mighty empire, spanning Siam (now Thailand), Burma (now Myanmar), Laos, and parts of Vietnam in the twelfth century of the Christian era, it shrank to an insignificant vassal state of both Siam and Vietnam until it was 'rescued' by France in the mid-nineteenth century, It finally emerged from colonial rule as a modern, independent nation state in the 1950s.

Independence, however, has never quelled Cambodians' fears of territorial and political domination by their two powerful neighbours. Disingenuous political leaders have been quick to exploit such fears, creating deep-seated prejudices against 'outsiders', particularly the Vietnamese minority in Cambodia.

Cambodia's location is also significant, lying as it does along a cultural fault-line between Chinese influence to the east and the 'Indianised' states of Thailand and Myanmar/Burma to the west. From India via these countries have come a pantheon of Hindu deities, Buddhism (now the official religion of Cambodia), Sanskrit, and the knowledge of how to grow paddy rice, Cambodia's staple food. From the east via Vietnam have come Chinese traders and entrepreneurs, who settled and gradually integrated into Cambodian society, bringing with them a razor-sharp business acumen. Yet throughout history, Cambodians have never blindly adopted ideas from outside, but, by a careful process of distillation, have adapted them to create their own unique, eclectic cultural identity.

The land shapes the people

Having regained land from Thailand, present-day Cambodia occupies an area of 180,000 sq km, roughly the size of England and Wales combined. It consists of a large, monotonously flat plain, which forms part of the lower Mekong Delta, enclosed on three sides by forested mountain ranges, creating a natural border with Thailand to the west and north, and Laos and Vietnam to the north and east. The fourth side, to the south, extending to the Gulf of Thailand, provides a gateway through which the Mekong, south-east Asia's 'Mother River', passes as it nears the end of its 4000-km journey from the chill Tibetan plateau to the warm waters of the China Sea. In the centre of the country is the Tonle Sap, or Great Lake, connected to the Mekong by a narrow channel of the same name.

Like history, land and climate have helped to shape the Cambodian people and their way of life. Two annual monsoons set the rhythm of rural

Nic Dunlop

▲ *Fishing boats on the Mekong river on the outskirts of Battambang town.*

life, based on rice farming and fishing: the hot, south-west monsoon, from May to October, brings heavy (but sometimes irregular) rain throughout the country. Farmers plant the main rain-fed rice crop as the rains begin, and harvest in November and December after the onset of the cool, dry monsoon winds from the north-east.

Monsoon rain and melting snow in the Himalayas produce a rise in the level of the Mekong – up to nine metres in places. The effect on the central plain is dramatic. Not only do the river and its tributaries burst their banks, flooding large areas, but the rise in the level of the river causes the waters of the Tonle Sap tributary (which flows into the Mekong during the dry season) to reverse their flow and head back upstream into the lake. The result is an amazing fivefold expansion in the size of the lake, which, at its fullest, covers nearly one-tenth of the country's surface area. As it expands, the nutrient-rich waters fertilise the paddy fields around its shores and feed the great shoals of fish, Cambodians' main source of protein, that spawn among the flooded fields before the lake empties back into the Mekong in November.

Around the edges of the sparsely wooded, watery plain, where the majority of Cambodians live, are the thinly populated mountain ranges, densely forested until a few years ago. In the south-west, around the exotically named Cardamom and Elephant Mountains, there are still large tracts of teak forest. In the west and north-east, virgin rainforest covers the lower reaches of the Dankret and Annam ranges, while lofty pines are found at higher elevations. Cambodia's other source of natural wealth lies in her deposits of rubies and sapphires, two of the world's most precious stones, found in particular around the western border town of Pailin. Until recently Pailin was an enclave of the Khmer Rouge, and the gem deposits were exploited not for the development of the country, but to buy arms to continue the devastating civil war.

The forests are also home to Cambodia's remaining fauna, including tigers, buffalo, elephants, wild oxen, clouded leopards, and bears, which are now much reduced in numbers following the war in the early 1970s.

Its topography and climate have made Cambodia predominantly a nation of farmers, fisherpeople, and foresters, deeply attached to the soil and water, fiercely independent, and, like most rural people, instinctively conservative – a tendency born of a rigidly hierarchical feudal past and the need to survive in a land where drought and flooding regularly deplete the rice crop. The French mistook this conservative streak for docility and an indifference to modernisation. Cambodian nationalists, protesting against French rule, repeatedly proved them wrong.

The Cambodians

More than 30 distinct ethnic groups make up the population of Cambodia. The largest group are the Khmer, constituting approximately 85 per cent of the populace. Historians are undecided about their origin: China, India, and island south-east Asia have all been suggested. However, it is known that 2000 years ago people speaking a language similar to modern Khmer had settled in the lower Mekong Delta. Living in the towns and villages of the plain, growing rice and fishing, the Khmer pride themselves on being the indigenous Cambodians, keeping alive the traditions and festivals of their powerful Khmer ancestors, worshipping the Lord Buddha, their culture steeped in popular Indo-Khmer mythology.

Despite enjoying political and economic strength in numbers, near-absorption of Cambodia by Thailand and Vietnam in the nineteenth century left the Khmer deeply suspicious of non-Khmer people, unfortunately for the other ethnic groups in Cambodia. The Vietnamese community, which may number as many as 500,000, is invariably the main target of racial animosity: following the 1998 elections, hatred of the 'Yuon', a derogatory term used for the Vietnamese, boiled over into violent, anti-Vietnamese demonstrations in Phnom Penh, the capital city. This was a disturbing reminder of the xenophobia whipped up by the regimes of both Lon Nol and Pol Pot, which decimated the Vietnamese community in the 1970s.

The other ethnic minorities may not attract the same animosity, but they are often treated as second-class citizens by the Khmer, though they may have lived in Cambodia for generations. The largest minority group, according to official figures, are the Cham. Estimated at 200,000 (the Cham themselves put the number at more than double the official figure), the Cham are descendants of the inhabitants of the medieval Hindu Kingdom of Champa, now part of Vietnam. Unlike the Khmer, who are mostly Buddhist, the Cham are Muslims. They adopted

▶ *Cham Muslim boys outside a mosque near Kompong Chhnang*

their faith from Malays who settled in southern Cambodia in the seventeenth century. They are traditionally cattle traders, butchers, and fisherpeople, catering for the Khmer, whose brand of Buddhism forbids them to slaughter animals. After the Cham come the Chinese, who have been gradually assimilated into Cambodian urban society, so that many Khmer townspeople have some Chinese blood. There are also small numbers of ethnic Thai and Lao.

Lastly, but of no less importance, are the 26 or so hill tribes, known collectively as the Khmer Loeu, or 'upland Khmer'. The six largest groups are the Kreung, Tampuan, Jarai, Stieng, Kuay, and Monong, each numbering approximately 10,000. In a more precarious situation are the 20 other tribes whose populations are estimated at below 3,000. The hill tribes, considered to be indigenous like the lowland Khmer, have traditionally lived in isolation, farming and fishing in the forests of north-east and south-west Cambodia. Over the past ten years, however, they have survived by clearing swathes of forest for plantations. The very survival of the Khmer Loeu is at risk.

Jim Holmes

▲ A member of the Kreung hill tribe in Toeun village, Ratanakiri. He wears the krema, the traditional cotton scarf of Cambodia.

▶ Monivong Boulevard, downtown Phnom Penh, with all the hustle and bustle of a modern south-east Asian city

Jim Holmes

Cambodia – the next Asian tiger?

Phnom Penh, Cambodia's capital city, seat of the monarchy and the Royal Government, is no longer the sleepy backwater of the early 1970s described in Jon Swain's haunting book, *River of Time*. With a population exceeding one million (and growing), it possesses all the trappings of a modern, bustling, south-east Asian city. Monivong Boulevard is the major thoroughfare in downtown Phnom Penh. It boasts futuristic, glass-fronted office blocks and rows of smart shops offering the latest electronic gadgetry. Brash, new hotels, restaurants, karaoke bars, and nightclubs offer round-the-clock entertainment. Sharp-dressed young men with mobile phones do business in street cafés before disappearing at speed behind the wheel of the latest model of Japanese car. And where 'cyclo' (tricycle) taxis once ruled the road, Honda mopeds now speed along the wide boulevards, dodging in and out of noisy, rush-hour traffic.

Though Cambodia is not in the same league as the 'tiger' economies of south-east Asia, figures for economic growth over the last ten years are impressive. According to the World Bank, Cambodia's growth measured an annual six per cent from 1991 to 1996, and inflation, which averaged 140 per cent per annum from 1990 to 1992 (due, in part, to the presence of 20,000 highly paid United Nations personnel), had stabilised at 3.5 per cent by 1995. The political crisis of mid-1997 slowed the growth rate significantly; nevertheless the government was predicting an upturn in economic activity and growth of 7 per cent by 2000, despite prospects of sluggish regional performance.

The business community of Phnom Penh and the other important commercial centres of Battambang and Kompong Som would probably share that optimism. A cheap labour-force and attractive incentives to invest have led to the spread of factories around Phnom Penh and elsewhere: factories producing garments, milled rice, cement, soft drinks, cigarettes and beer, for a society hungry for consumer goods after the lean years of the 1970s and 1980s.

Statistics, however, often belie the reality. Economic prosperity has come to a minority of Cambodians, but the majority find themselves excluded from a share of the spoils. While government policy has encouraged private enterprise, little, if anything, has been done to alleviate poverty for an estimated 40 per cent of the population, most of whom live in rural areas – although urban poverty is now increasing at a faster rate, as poor people from the countryside migrate to the towns to escape the prevailing lack of health-care facilities, secondary schools, electricity, running water, and decent roads. Investment in irrigation would greatly increase the rice yield, but this too is neglected, making Cambodia's average annual rice yield one of the lowest in the region.

Six Cambodian families adapting to a changing world

Not far from the bright lights of Monivong Boulevard in Phnom Penh is Bondos Vichea. This former wasteland is now home to 300 squatter families, among them Kim Vanna, her husband, Chea Savou, and their nine children. The capital city's rising tide of prosperity has passed them by. They live in a two-roomed shack without sanitation or water, existing on the meagre wages that Savou earns as a street barber. They have just discovered that the Bondos Vichea site has been sold by the government to a property developer. But the residents are planning to fight the eviction ...

On the outskirts of Phnom Penh, among the shifting masses of migrant workers, lives Sey Samon with her two children. Samon was a casual labourer at a cement factory, until her former husband beat her up so savagely that she miscarried the child she was expecting. Samon almost died too. Increasing domestic violence is an ugly by-product of a society where women, through necessity, make up the majority of the work force. Some men feel threatened and are lashing out. This book will show how Samon and other women are responding to the problem.

One hundred and fifty kilometres north of Phnom Penh is the town of Kompong Chhnang, set on the banks of the Tonle Sap, close to the southern tip of the Great Lake. Upstream in Kompong Kros village, a collection of floating houses, live Chea Rith, his wife Chenda Mach and two of their four children. Rith and Mach are Cham fisherpeople and followers of Islam. A mosque on stilts stands nearby. Rith manages to find time every Friday to pray. The rest of the week he and his wife are fishing – for ever-smaller catches. It is a worrying trend, more so for them because they have no plot of land to rely on. Why are catches getting smaller in one of the world's richest fishing grounds?

Four hundred kilometres north-west of the capital is the province of Battambang, the traditional 'rice basket' of Cambodia. Not far from the provincial capital are the villages of Takorm and Chisang, home to Chhoun Yeath and her children, and Mong Bora, Mot Savate, and their children respectively. Village life seems a world apart from the sophisticated city life enjoyed by the urbanites of Phnom Penh. The gap between urban wealth and rural poverty is stark. Both families survive by growing rice and vegetables on small plots of land, fishing, and whatever casual labour they can find during the dry season. Yeath is fearful of losing her plot to speculators, now that land can be freely bought and sold. Bora and Savate live with a different fear: that of treading on a landmine every time they and their children step outside the house. They actually live in a suspected minefield, the dreadful legacy of three decades of conflict. Bora has already lost a leg to a mine.

Chhoun Yeath

Mong Bora

Chea Rith and Chenda Mach

Kim Sopheap

THAILAND

LAOS

Banteay Meanchey

Siem Reap

Preah Vihear

Ratanakiri

Stung Treng

Battambang

Battambang

Tonle Sap

Kompong Thom

Mekong River

Mondulkiri

Pursat

Kompong Chhnang

Kratie

Kompong Cham

Phnom Penh

Prey Veng

Koh Kong

Kompong Speu

Kandal

Svay Rieng

VIETNAM

Kampot

Takeo

Gulf of Thailand

0   200 kilometres

0   100 miles

Chea Savou

Sey Samon

On the other side of Cambodia, close to the border with Vietnam, in Ratanakiri province, live Tep Seng, his wife, Kim Sopheap, and their four children. They are members of the Kreung hill tribe, the first humans to resettle the earth following a devastating fire, according to tribal legend. The Kreung are forest people, clearing areas for rice cultivation, but also harvesting the trees and plants for fruit, vegetables, building materials, and medicine. The forests hold profound spiritual significance for the animist hill tribes, but their beliefs are being crudely trampled by the logging companies, for whom the trees mean nothing but enormous profits. And for the past decade, the loggers have enjoyed a bonanza. The hill tribes, meanwhile, have lost some ground, literally, but are fighting back.

▼ *Cambodians are sceptical of government promises to sweep away corruption and spend more on social services*

Mike Goldwater

Tackling injustice in Cambodia today

Hun Sen, re-elected Prime Minister in 1998, presides over the changing state of Cambodian society. He and his government are aware of the growing inequalities and have vowed to increase public spending on social welfare and health care. A pledge has been made to reduce military spending, and Hun Sen has resigned as commander-in-chief of the armed forces in an attempt to emphasise their neutrality. Cambodians remain sceptical of government promises. Injustice is still at the heart of Cambodian society today, as it always has been – manifested in government corruption, a judiciary whose integrity is questionable, widespread disregard for human rights, and ill treatment of women. Cambodians want the government to tackle these fundamental problems above all else.

The history of Cambodia

Linking the past to the present

In the life-story of any nation, the past is never far from the present. Thus it becomes all the more crucial to our understanding of the present that we have a grasp of what went before. David Chandler, the eminent historian, identifies three common and still distinct threads running through the complex fabric of Cambodian history. The first is the 'pervasiveness of patronage', emanating from a rigid and conservative social hierarchy. Linked to this is Chandler's second theme, the myth of the 'change-lessness' and the implied 'backwardness' of Cambodian society – a myth invented by the Thais and Vietnamese, reinforced by the French, and perpetuated by autocratic Cambodian leaders. The third theme is Cambodia's location between Thailand and Vietnam and its proximity to powerful China.

Jim Holmes

> ### MYTHICAL BEGINNINGS
>
> An Indian Brahman called Kaundinya appeared one day off the shore of a distant country. A *nagi*, or dragon princess, whose father was king of the waterlogged land, took a boat and paddled out to meet him. Kaundinya took up his magical bow and shot an arrow into her boat, frightening her into marrying him. Before the wedding, Kaundinya gave her clothes and, in return, the dragon king enlarged the territory to be given to his future son-in-law, by drinking up the water that covered the land. After the wedding the king built them a great city and changed the name of the country to Kambuja.

The Brahman bridegroom in the story is India; the watery country which becomes his home is Cambodia; the myth is an expression of the depth of Indian influence on Cambodia. The importance of Indian influence cannot be underestimated during the early centuries of the Christian era: Cambodia, then probably a loose collection of petty fiefdoms along the coast of the Mekong delta, known first as 'Funan' and thereafter 'Chenla' by the Chinese, became a stopover point along the main trade route between India and China. Over time, Indian traders and travellers brought ideas and technology that the Khmer shaped to suit their own environment: wet-land rice growing; a writing system; Hinduism, followed by Buddhism; and the idea of universal kingship.

Tourists at Wat Phnom, a Buddhist temple founded in 1372, according to legend by a woman called Penh

The rise and fall of the Khmer empire: 9th to 15th century

In the year 802, King Jayavarman II took part in a ritual ceremony that installed him as the universal monarch of a state whose borders are described by an inscription as *'China, Champa, the ocean, and the land of cardamoms and mangoes (in the west)'*. How such a powerful entity came about in the first place remains a mystery. Jayavarman chose to rule his kingdom from Angkor, near the present-day town of Siem Riep, north of the Tonle Sap. Angkor was to remain the capital and symbol of the mighty empire for six hundred years. Although it was to fall into decline, its greatness lives on, symbolised as it is by the image of the great Angkor Wat temple on the Cambodian national flag.

The kings of Angkor were avid builders. On their numerous temples and palaces were carved inscriptions in Sanskrit and Khmer, and elaborate bas-reliefs from which we can catch glimpses of what life was like for the inhabitants of the imperial city in a highly stratified society, where the various social classes were joined in a patron–client relationship. At the apex was the god-king, who would identify himself with one of the Hindu deities to establish his authority as 'ruler of the entire world which he had conquered ... even steadier than the sun which occasionally was distant'. The use of religion both to reinforce and demonstrate political power is clearly shown by the twelfth-century construction of the world's largest religious complex: the temple, observatory, and tomb of Angkor Wat.

Below the monarch were his functionaries: ministers, generals, astronomers, and others, on whom were bestowed patronage – land, wealth, and titles – in return for loyalty. All land remained the property of the king, a tradition that continued, in theory at least, until French occupation in the mid-nineteenth century.

At the bottom of the social scale were tradeswomen (it was women who took charge of trade, according to Chou Ta-Kuan, a thirteenth-century Chinese emissary to Cambodia), farm labourers, and slaves, who worked the land for their feudal masters. Records show that rice was harvested two or three times a year, thanks to a complex irrigation system, long since abandoned. Bas-reliefs also indicate that farmers' tools, clothing, and stilted houses changed little until the arrival of the French.

The Khmer empire reached its apogee at the end of the twelfth century, during the reign of Jayavarman VII, a relatively enlightened monarch, who is credited with a number of public works, including hospitals, roads, and bridges. After his death came steady decline and gradual loss of territory to Siam, ending in the capture of Angkor from the Khmer in the 1431. Cambodia's Golden Age was over. Its memory would be invoked more than five hundred years later by Pol Pot, the murderous leader of the Khmer Rouge, who abused Angkor's ancient splendours to whip up racism and xenophobia, rather than to instil national pride.

Jim Holmes

◄ *Cambodia's Golden Age came to an end nearly 600 years ago.*

The dark ages: 15th to 19th century

The fall of Angkor ushered in four hundred years of political and territorial domination by Siam and Vietnam. Land was occupied by Vietnam to the east and Siam to the west, while an ever-shrinking, politically weakened centre served as a buffer zone between the two mutually suspicious powers. Cambodia's geographical location had become important, and to this day it is seen as a buffer state by the Thais and Vietnamese, as demonstrated by the interventions of both powers in Cambodian affairs during the 1970s and 1980s.

As a consequence of Siamese and Vietnamese occupation, Cambodia was at risk of literally disappearing from the map by the mid-nineteenth century. In desperation, King Norodom asked the French to intervene and save his country. They duly obliged, declaring Cambodia a French protectorate in 1864, after years of unofficial contact via missionaries and explorers.

French rule: from protectorate to colony, 1864 to 1953

Like Vietnam and Siam, who saw themselves as the 'mother' and 'father' of their Cambodian 'child', the French viewed Cambodia as a backward, unchanging country, her people docile, immune to modernisation and in need of the *mission civilisatrice* that France was also undertaking in Vietnam and Laos. 'Civilising mission' was a euphemism for the sacrifice of Cambodia's development to further French commercial and political interests – no different from the aims of other nineteenth-century European colonial powers. France's enduring legacy to Cambodia was the 1884 Land Act, which legitimised private ownership of land for the first time and allowed French companies to turn large areas of common land into profitable rubber plantations. Deforestation had begun. Taxes raised were spent on keeping the staff of the colonial administration in comfort and style, rather than on health care and education for Cambodians, who were effectively paying to be exploited. The French justified the lack of investment in education by claiming dishonestly that Cambodians themselves did not want schools and colleges.

Not surprisingly, anti-French feeling grew among Cambodians, who also objected to the presence of Vietnamese brought in by the French to assist them. There was nationwide unrest in 1885, and in 1916 40,000 peasants passed through Phnom Penh to protest against the onerous tax burden imposed on them by the French administration. In 1925, Felix Bardez, a French official, was killed by villagers who were also protesting against high taxes. The myth of Cambodians as 'docile', 'backward' people had been shattered.

By the Second World War, French control in Indo-China was weak, and pro-independence movements in the region were getting stronger. France managed to cling to its colonies after the war, but, worn down by military defeats in the region, finally agreed to Cambodian independence in 1953.

▲ *Portraits of the King and Queen are commonly displayed in shops and offices: a mark of popular respect for the monarchy, despite the King's frequent absences from Cambodia.*

From order to chaos, peace to war: 1953 to 1975

It had taken more than five hundred years for Cambodia to regain her independence. There was to be no return to the glorious past of Angkor, but Cambodians rejoiced in the presence of King Norodom Sihanouk, their latter-day god-king, whose political manoeuvrings had helped to bring foreign rule to an end.

As monarch, however, Sihanouk was restricted by the constitution to a non-political role, so he abdicated in 1955 to pursue his political ambitions, founding a national political movement, the *Sangkum Reastr Niyum*, or People's Socialist Community. In elections in the same year, Sihanouk's party took three-quarters of the vote and won all the seats in the national assembly. He was certainly a popular leader, but his victory was also a result of vote-rigging and intimidation of political rivals. Forty-three years on, similar charges were made against Prime Minister Hun Sen and his party. How far has Cambodia moved along the road towards democracy?

Sihanouk, the autocratic patriarch, governed Cambodia for 15 years. He was a populist, who enjoyed nothing better than touring the country and speaking to ordinary Cambodians. His idiosyncratic brand of 'Buddhist socialism' meant high expenditure on education for all, but also economic mismanagement and corruption, bringing prosperity to an urban elite and a gradual decline in living standards for most people.

Sihanouk's downfall came as the economic situation deteriorated, and opposition within his own party grew. However, it was finally precipitated by events in neighbouring Vietnam, where civil war had broken out between North and South in the early 1960s. Once again, Cambodia's location was to play a crucial role in the subsequent turn of events. History was repeating itself. Believing that the Vietnamese National Liberation Front (NLF), allied to the communist regime in Hanoi, would win, Sihanouk backed it. As fighting intensified and the USA, supporting South Vietnam, increased its bombing of targets in the north, the NLF took to using a supply route, known as the Ho Chi Minh Trail, which ran through Laos and Cambodia into South Vietnam. The US objected to the NLF presence on Cambodian soil and, illegally, began bombing eastern and central Cambodia, killing an estimated 150,000 Cambodians between 1969 and 1973. By then, Sihanouk had been ousted by Marshal Lon Nol, his pro-America former Commander-in-Chief, in a *coup d'état* in 1970. How far the US government was involved in the coup remains unclear.

Lon Nol could do little to stem the rising economic and social crisis in the country. Beleaguered in Phnom Penh, his government was under increasing attack from a group of communist insurgents, the 'Khmer Rouge', or 'Red Khmer', as they were labelled by Sihanouk, who had earlier outlawed them. US bombing, a widening gap between the urban rich and rural poor, and the knowledge that their exiled king was now backing the Khmer Rouge drove those in the countryside into the arms of the communists, who preached social equality and an end to corruption. With growing support from the Cambodian people and arms from China and North Vietnam, the Khmer Rouge, led by the enigmatic Pol Pot, pressed towards Phnom Penh. On 17 April 1975, Khmer Rouge footsoldiers, many of them young, clad in black cotton pyjamas, marched into the capital. Almost immediately orders were given to the residents to evacuate the city. This was Day One of Democratic Kampuchea. Year Zero of the Revolution. The clock was to be turned back to an age without money, organised education, religion, and books. The firestorm was about to begin ...

▼ *Skulls found in caves used as a torture and execution centre by the Khmer Rouge*

Mike Goldwater

Life under the Khmer Rouge: 1975 to 1979

Youk Chhang, now director of the Documentation Centre of Cambodia, which conducts research into Khmer Rouge atrocities, was home alone in Phnom Penh on 17 April 1975. His mother and sister had gone out for the day. He was 14. 'I was terrified when I saw the young Khmer Rouge soldiers,' he says. 'They screamed at me to get out of my house, so I went. I walked for

Nic Dunlop

▲ *A few of the thousands of people tortured and murdered by the Khmer Rouge at the old High School in Phnom Penh*

two weeks to my mother's village. On the way I found myself in the middle of the road. It was raining heavily. There were dark clouds around me. I couldn't see. I had nowhere to turn. I was utterly alone and afraid. I will never forget that feeling.'

He was eventually re-united with his mother and sister, and the three were sent to Battambang. Later he witnessed the killing of a young couple whose crime was to fall in love. 'I was called to a meeting in Preah Neth Preah village. A young man and woman were brought before the crowd, tied to a pole and blindfolded. The Khmer Rouge soldier told us that they had fallen in love without the permission of *Angkar* and asked what should happen to them. People began to shout: "Crush them, crush them, kill, kill". The soldier took a thick bamboo stick and hit the man repeatedly on his head and body. Blood flowed from his mouth and nose. Once the man stopped moving, the soldier removed the blindfold from the woman. She was very pale. Her eyes were closed. The soldier hit the woman until she, too, no longer moved. They were not dead, but were buried alive near the local temple.'

Chhang and his mother survived the cataclysm, finding their way over the Thai border to a refugee camp in early 1979, following the ousting of the Khmer Rouge by an invading Vietnamese army. Chhang's sister and an estimated 1.7 million Cambodians – almost one quarter of the population – did not survive. They died from starvation, exhaustion, disease, and execution.

People were killed because they fell in love. How were so many lives lost and so much suffering wrought on an entire population in such a brief time? Nothing short of a complete transformation of society was the aim of Pol Pot and his zealous Khmer Rouge comrades. They had been hatching their extreme version of socialist revolution since their student days in France in the 1950s and, thereafter, during years of isolation in the jungles of eastern Cambodia. Their ideology was a radical blend of Maoism, with its emphasis on collectivisation and national self-sufficiency, and rabid chauvinism, directed principally against Vietnam. On paper, they wanted to abolish all vestiges of a corrupt and unequal Cambodia and return the country to a classless, agrarian society. They talked about liberating the rural poor.

The reality, however, was different from the rhetoric. The increasingly paranoid Khmer Rouge leadership was interested in destroying rather than building society, and controlling rather than liberating the population. People educated under the *ancien régime* – doctors, engineers, and teachers, known as 'new people' or 'April 17 people' – were singled out as 'class enemies' and systematically culled. Only 50 out of 500 doctors survived; 5000 out of 20,000 teachers. New people became used to the chilling Khmer Rouge mantra: *'Keeping you is no profit; losing you is no loss'*. Ethnic minorities and political opponents, real or imaginary, were targeted with equal ruthlessness. Up to 100,000 Vietnamese may have been killed. This was genocide.

Family life was destroyed. Families were split up, and a system of communal living, working, and eating was introduced. The sinister *Angkar* became the supposed fount of all care and support for every Cambodian. Individuality was destroyed. People all wore identical clothes, ate the same food, did the same back-breaking work, underwent the same political education. Personal freedom was replaced by total control by *Angkar*, 'the pineapple' – so called because it had eyes everywhere. Control was through punishment, torture, and death for those who failed to suppress their individuality.

Customs, traditions, money, religion, books, newspapers, cinema, and theatre were all abolished. Public buildings such as schools, colleges, and hospitals were emptied and left derelict. Libraries were scattered. Factories, houses, shops, and valuable infrastructure were abandoned by virtue of having been built before 'Year Zero'. Some Buddhist temples were destroyed. There was little laughter or joy in Democratic Kampuchea. Days consisted of twelve-hour shifts in the rice fields, punctuated by meagre rations of food and gruelling sessions of political indoctrination. There were no holidays. People died of overwork.

Towards the end there were uprisings in the east to protest against Khmer Rouge excesses, but it was the anti-Vietnamese racism of the Pol Pot regime that ultimately led to its downfall. Cambodian attacks on Vietnamese border towns and villages, and reports of the decimation of the Vietnamese community brought a decisive response. On 25 December 1978 a Vietnamese force of 120,000 entered Cambodia, reaching Phnom Penh on 7 January 1979. The 'enemy' was back, but the nightmare was over. Or was it?

▲ *Prasat Ek Phnom, a ruined temple used as a prison by Pol Pot's forces*

Nic Dunlop

Rebuilding Cambodia: 1979 onwards

The twenty years since the end of Democratic Kampuchea have not brought the peace and stability that the Cambodian people craved. During the 1980s the Vietnamese-backed People's Republic of Kampuchea (PRK) was isolated by an economic embargo slapped on it by the US, Chinese, and western European governments – including the UK – still smarting over Soviet-backed North Vietnam's recent victory over the South. With cruel and scarcely credible irony, the USA and other Western powers ignored genuine hardship inside Cambodia, while giving financial assistance to the Coalition Government of Democratic Kampuchea (CGDK), the Thai-based opposition movement, whose dominant faction was none other than the repugnant Khmer Rouge.

As the Khmer Rouge rebuilt their military machine, the PRK government did its best to restore some semblance of normality to a

ក្ដី Nic Dunlop

▲ *Battambang, 1992: 20,000 soldiers and personnel belonging to the United Nations Transitional Authority in Cambodia (UNTAC) were charged with securing peace and free and fair elections.*

traumatised population and a shattered economy, with limited assistance from the Soviet Union and other eastern-bloc countries. Progress was hindered by incursions into the country by a re-armed Khmer Rouge and the other factional forces of the CGDK. It finally became clear to all sides, other than the Khmer Rouge, that only a political solution could bring lasting peace. A deal was eventually brokered, stipulating the withdrawal of all Vietnamese troops in preparation for a comprehensive peace agreement. The Paris Peace Accords were finally signed in 1991 by the Cambodian government and the three factions of the CGDK – the Khmer Rouge, the *Armée Nationale Sihanoukiste*, headed by the former King Sihanouk, and the anti-Communist Khmer People's National Liberation Front – who were to take part in elections, overseen by the United Nations Transitional Authority in Cambodia (UNTAC) in 1993. Once more the international community deferred to the Khmer Rouge, preferring to close its eyes to the clear evidence of genocide, for the sake of political expediency.

The elections took place without the Khmer Rouge, who withdrew and subsequently did their best to disrupt voting. The UN operation cost an estimated two billion US dollars and attracted much criticism, but a coalition government did, nevertheless, emerge in relatively free and fair polls, though not without the aid of a UN-brokered deal between the two main parties: the United National Front for an Independent, Neutral, Peaceful and Co-operative Cambodia (known by its French acronym FUNCINPEC), led by Prince Norodom Ranariddh, King Sihanouk's son, and the Cambodia People's Party (CPP), headed by Hun Sen.

Could Cambodia now finally put her tragic past behind her and look to a brighter future? The question is still in the balance, although there is more optimism than ever before that peace will prevail. The Khmer Rouge appear to be a spent force. Pol Pot is dead, his jungle encampment in Anlong Veng now in government hands, his troops under the control of the Cambodian armed forces.

The fight against poverty goes on, however, and must be taken seriously by subsequent administrations. One of the reasons why the Khmer Rouge were able to take power in the first place was that they received support from a disenchanted rural population, who were ignored by government and exploited by a land-owning elite. The current government ignores rural discontentment at its peril. The lesson of the Cambodian past is that history has the tragic habit of repeating itself.

Rural livelihoods at risk

Paddy-rice farming in the north-west

Jim Holmes

▲ *Chhoun Yeath waters her plot of land. The vegetables will be sold at market to provide cash for food, medicine, and school fees.*

It is November in Takorm, a small village of Khmer rice farmers in Battambang Province. The air is dry and hot. The village is an island in a shimmering sea of lime-green fields. The mathematical monotony of the horizon is broken by spindly coconut palms. Chhoun Yeath waters the vegetable patch next to her small house, raised off the ground on stilts. Her daughter cooks lunch on the open wood stove beneath the house. Yeath is preparing to harvest her one rice crop of the year, planted at the beginning of the rainy season in May. Without access to irrigation, she relies on the monsoon rain. However, this year there has been insufficient rain and, like other Cambodian farmers, Yeath knows that she will have a poor crop again – possibly only half as much as she would normally harvest. After paying her debt to the local rice-lender, there probably will not be enough rice left to feed her four children during the year. But although rice provides on average three-quarters of their food, Yeath and her family have never depended on the rice crop to provide all their needs, because they cannot rely on adequate rainfall. So she uses a number of strategies to feed and support the family. She and her children fish in the nearby river, in their own paddy field, and in the pond beside the local pagoda. She grows her own vegetables. Once a week during the dry season, Yeath makes a four-hour round trip to the forest to collect grass, from which she weaves floor-mats for sale. Money earned from the mats and from occasional casual labour enables her to pay for medicine and to send her children to school, as well as buying extra food.

By Cambodian standards, Yeath and her family figure among the 43 per cent of rural people who fall below the poverty line. However, by combining farming, fishing, and collecting a variety of products in the forest, they manage to subsist.

Swidden farming in the forests of the east

In a cleared area, surrounded by dense bushes, one kilometre from their home village of Toeun in Ratanakiri, Tep Seng, deputy village leader, and his wife, Kim Sopheap, both of the Kreung tribe, are taking a break from harvesting to eat a lunch of rice and *prahok* (fish paste) with their children in a small shelter next to their field. During the rice harvest, the tribespeople spend most of their time living next to their fields, so they can work longer hours during the day and protect the crop from hungry animals at night. Like the other tribes in the uplands, the Kreung practise swidden farming, growing upland rice – as opposed to the paddy-rice farming of the lowland plain – and a variety of other crops. Swidden agriculture is based on the rotational use of several plots of land by one family: land in the forest is cleared, and rice or another crop is planted. The family farm the plot for up to four years, depending on the fertility of the soil, before moving to a different one. By moving from plot to plot, they never exhaust the soils. The forest is able to reclaim the fallow land and regenerate it for future use.

▼ *The hill tribes use forest products for building materials. Leaves are woven together to form a water-tight roof.*

Jim Holmes

The tribespeople depend on the forest for much more than agricultural land. Seng explains: 'The forest provides all our needs. We take the wood of the *Koki* tree to make the floor of our houses, *Churtiel* and bamboo for the walls, and grass, bamboo, and leaves for the roof. The forest is also full of fruit, leaves, and vegetables that we eat. It used to be home to wild animals such as tortoises and lizards that were a source of food. And we have the rivers, which give us fish.' The Kreung use some medicinal plants, but rely predominantly on animal sacrifices to cure illnesses.

The forest is home to the *alak*, the spirits that protect it. Seng continues: 'The spirits live in the trees, streams, paths, and fields. When certain trees are cut, the spirits get angry and can inflict harm not only on those cutting the trees, but also on those who stand by and allow the trees to be cut. The spirits bring rain for us, but can also cause drought and make us go mad or lose our way in the forest. They are very powerful, and in order to keep them contented, we sacrifice buffaloes, cows, and other animals to them.'

Like Yeath and her family, Seng, Kim and their children need the forest and the rivers to continue their way of life.

Fishing in the rivers and lakes of the north

Chenda Mach and her husband, Chea Rith, the Cham fisherpeople, differ from Yeath, Seng, and Kim, in that they rely solely on fishing to make a living. They bought a boat, equipped with an outboard engine, two years ago and use it every day of the year, apart from Muslim holy days. The boat cost £300, most of which was borrowed from a Chinese trader at a very high annual interest rate of 75 per cent. Mach and Rith still owe nearly £60. Where they fish depends on the season: during the wet season, they travel north from their village to the Tonle Sap, where the fish begin to spawn in the submerged forest and shrublands bordering the lake; during the dry season, the fish migrate from the lake to the Mekong, so Mach and Rith lay their nets nearer home on the river, to catch what they can. The daily catch is between 1.5 and 5 kilograms. The family – Mach and Rith have four children, two of whom stay with grandparents in order to be nearer school – keeps one kilo to eat, and the rest is sold on to a trader. The money they make is used mainly to buy rice and vegetables and fuel for the boat. What is left is for repairs to the boat and the nets. There is little left for anything else. In an emergency money always has to be borrowed, always at a high price.

▲ *Chea Rith, Chenda Mach, and their children set out on a fishing trip.*

Struggling to subsist

Since the end of the 1980s, Cambodia has changed dramatically. Rural people have had to adapt to the rules of the free market, which, while allowing them to sell their produce as and when they want, also exposes them to powerful and often hostile economic forces. Rural people are finding it difficult to work in the new economic order.

Fish stocks are dwindling ...

In the past, the husband and wife team of Mach and Rith supplemented their daily catch by rearing fish in a bamboo cage beneath the house. They also used to process some of the fresh fish into *prahok* and dried, salted fish, but this year they have been able to do neither. Rith explains why: 'Catches have been going down for the past five years or so. And not only is the quantity of fish we catch less, but the fish of certain species seem to be getting smaller.' According to him, the main reason for the smaller catch is over-fishing by illegal methods. 'Many fishermen use a motor attached to a car battery to produce an electric current, which kills the fish. In addition, it's possible to buy nets with a very fine mesh, which catch the fry before they have matured. And some use the charge from landmines to create an explosion in the water.'

Across the river from Rith and Mach's village, spanning a parallel channel of the Tonle Sap River, is a net, 350 metres wide, draped over a bamboo frame. The net has three 'corridors' pointing downstream, which taper into large bamboo cages. This is 'lot no. 9', one of nearly 300 river and lake fishing lots in Cambodia, covering an area of nearly 10,000 square kilometres. Sach In and his wife, Nguon Sem, beat their competitors with a bid of £50,000 for lot no. 9 for two years. In expects to catch 800 tons over the two-year period and make a final profit of approximately £65,000, which is less than he has made previously. He agrees with Rith and Mach that fish stocks have diminished over the last few years, but is quick to deny that the exploitation of the commercial fishing lots is a cause. He also insists that the mesh of the nets is wide

▶ *Fishing for subsistence on the Tonle Sap river near Kompong Chhnang*

Jim Holmes

enough to allow the fry to pass through. As he speaks, a gate at the mouth of one of the corridors opens, and fish are washed down towards the bamboo cage. They are minute. 'We use the small fish as food for the larger ones,' he admits.

Rith and Mach may not agree that diminishing fish stocks have nothing to do with the commercial fishing lots, though they say nothing, perhaps fearful of speaking out against a powerful businessman. Whatever the reason, the increase in the number of fishing lots is, without doubt, denying access for subsistence fisherpeople to large areas of river and lake. Their livelihoods are at risk. 'We are going to slip back into more debt. That's for sure,' says Mach.

... and forests are for sale

Just as subsistence fisherpeople are being prevented from using traditional fishing grounds, due to the presence of commercial fishing lots, so the hill tribes of Ratanakiri and elsewhere have seen extensive logging concessions granted to commercial companies, individuals, and army officers by the

Cambodian government – often illegally, according to independent organisations, such as Global Witness, which monitor the situation. The Cambodian Forestry Department estimates that there are approximately 50,000 sq km of forest under concession, representing more than half of Cambodia's remaining forest. In January 1999, concessions covering 20,000 sq km were terminated, but these were areas that had already been logged out, according to Global Witness. The concessions invariably encompass land traditionally used by the local tribespeople.

The loggers have been coming to Toeun to take logs and to establish plantations since the mid-1980s. One is a Kreung member of Cambodia's armed forces, Long, who was born in Toeun village. 'He is doing this for his own interests,' says Tep Seng. 'Long believes in the customs of the tribe, but he wants to be rich. And many young people are following his example.' Long has become rich, compared with his fellow Kreung. One metre cubed of top-quality *Churtiel* or *Koki* wood fetches up to £20 at a sawmill in Banlung, the provincial capital of Ratanakiri, and trees can grow up to 20 metres high. On the commercial market, one metre cubed is sold on for up to £300. By contrast, Seng estimates his family's total annual income at £30.

In late 1998 a foreign company began sending trucks to the forest. The loggers have widened the road to make way for them. At a nearby clearing where they are working, huge trees lie in the red mud, waiting to be removed to Banlung for sawing. Farther into the denuded forest, saplings have been broken by falling trees, and the ground is gashed where trees have been dragged to the roadside. 'The spirits are angry with the loggers and with us for not protecting the forest,' says Seng. 'The animals have disappeared, and the spirits have caused a drought that is harming our crops and reducing our fish catches. If they carry on cutting the trees, the Kreung will die, and the world will be destroyed.'

Environmental devastation – upsetting the natural balance

The World Bank recently estimated that within three to five years Cambodia's forests will have been commercially logged out. The effects will be far-reaching and incalculable. The loss of mature trees is already damaging Cambodia's lakesides and riversides: cutting the trees means removing the roots that help to keep the soil in place; without the roots, the soil is washed away in heavy rain into streams, rivers, and lakes, which gradually become silted up. Silt damages the spawning grounds of fish, and so fish stocks decrease ... and diminishing fish stocks make life harder for Rith and Mach in Kompong Chhnang. The tribespeople are convinced also that the loss of forest has caused drought. So Yeath in Battambang may be suffering poor harvests because of the deforestation.

There will be further pressure on the environment and rural communities if the Cambodian government goes ahead with plans to construct a number of hydro-electric dams on the river Mekong and its tributaries. Thailand, Laos, Vietnam, and China have all taken advantage of the river, and the Asian Development Bank is pressing Cambodia to follow suit. The dams will generate electricity, though the cost is unknown, and a proportion of the power may go for export to Thailand. But how are dams likely to affect the environment and the people living there? The results of studies by environmental groups are not positive: it is likely that the dams will reduce downstream river flows, which, in turn, will deliver less nutrient-rich alluvium to agricultural land. The reservoirs created at the sites of some of the proposed dams will flood rivers, forests, fields, and villages. Large numbers of people will be displaced. Their world will be destroyed.

Land rights – the crucial issue

In the past, the villagers of Toeun were able to rely on the forest for their material and spiritual survival, because each village had enough communal land for cultivation, foraging, and hunting. Land does not belong to any one individual, but is entrusted to the tribal ancestors, whose authority rests with the village elders. Unfortunately for the hill tribes, their way of managing the land does not accord with the current land laws, which fail to recognise communal land rights. And without guaranteed right of access to the forest, duly respected by all, especially politicians and business people, the Kreung will not be able to maintain their traditional way of life.

Land rights are crucial not only to the hill tribes affected by logging, but to all poor farmers throughout Cambodia, whose land is their only capital. Yeath and her husband acquired their two-hectare plot in 1979. Under current legislation, she is the rightful owner of the land, having occupied it for more than five years, but she still has no certificate of ownership. Instead, she relies on a hand-written letter from the local authorities. Yeath remains hopeful that her land will never be taken from her. However, evidence over the last 15 years shows that rural people, often illiterate and unable to pay corrupt officials for the necessary documentation, are losing their land and, along with it, their livelihoods. Their basic rights of access to land are not being respected. In the past, low

▼ 'If the logging companies carry on cutting the trees, the Kreung will die, and the world will be destroyed' – Tep Seng, village leader, Ratanakiri Province

population density and a non-commercial relationship with land meant that it was in plentiful supply and relatively evenly distributed, most families having at least one hectare. Now a rising population, coupled with uncontrolled logging, the increased use of land for commercial plantations, and the ever-greedier demands of land speculators, has produced both increasing landlessness among rural people – estimated at 15 per cent and rising – and greater inequality of land distribution. To put it simply, there are more people without land, and more people with less land than before. And together these factors can only create more poverty.

Debt, most frequently incurred to meet the high cost of health care, is a major reason why rural households are losing their land. In the absence of a national institution offering credit at a realistic price to farmers, they have no choice but to borrow rice and money from commercial lenders at exorbitant rates of interest. Even farmers with access to rice banks, such as Yeath, may still be obliged to take out loans on the commercial market. The commercial lenders are always careful to secure land as collateral. If the farmer then suffers a bad harvest, he or she has no choice but to sell land to settle the debt.

Fighting back ...

Extensive deforestation, dwindling fish stocks, and growing landlessness make it difficult for anyone to predict a better future for Cambodia's rural poor. They, however, are determined to create a more secure life for their children. And that means confronting those who wield power.

The villagers of Toeun have been taking direct action against the logging companies for several years. In 1996 they stopped the trucks *en route* to the forest and confiscated three chainsaws from the loggers; they have forced the local authorities to compensate them for the damage done to the forest, and have obtained £650 from Mr Long, the Kreung businessman. However, they still face the fundamental problem of ensuring access to their traditional land.

Nearby, the Kreung villagers of Krola are addressing this issue, which for them dates back to 1993 after the elections, when local townspeople went on a land-grabbing spree within the customary borders of the village. In 1998 Krola became the first village in Cambodia to request a communal land title from the government. Help in drafting the request came from a local NGO called the Non-Timber Forest Products Project, based in Banlung. Villagers are aware that their chances of success are slender, more so because much of the village land falls within a 600 sq km concession granted to Hero, a powerful Taiwanese logging company. Nevertheless, they are determined to fight for their rights. 'Even if the government does not grant us the communal land title, we will mobilise every villager to protect the boundary of this village. We will never give up our right to live as we want to live,' asserts Bun Choun, the head of the Village Development Committee of Krola.

The inhabitants of Takorm village in Battambang have also joined forces to guard against losing their land – in their case by tackling the problem of debt. With some initial help from Oxfam in 1992, the villagers established a rice bank. Six years later, there are 96 family members benefiting from the scheme, which allows them to borrow rice when they need it, and pay back after the harvest at a rate of interest of 20 per cent, which is a fraction of that levied by the commercial rice-lender. Crucially, defaulting on the loan from the rice bank does not mean the loss of land. The scheme relies on social pressure from other members to ensure that people honour their loan commitments. The villagers have also formed a cow bank, whereby a family tends the adult animal and keeps the calves for ploughing, thus avoiding the need to rent a draught animal.

Chea Rith and Chenda Mach, the fisherpeople from Kompong Chhnang, are less fortunate, in that they are not members of a solidarity group that could campaign for government action on the issues of falling fish stocks and illegal fishing methods, or a self-help group that could provide credit facilities. Their future is doubly vulnerable, because they do not have any land to farm if they are unable to make fishing pay. So far they have not resorted to using illegal fishing methods to increase their catch. If the situation does not improve, however, there may be no option: they have four children to feed, clothe, and send to school.

Asking for a fair deal

Rural people are not rooted immutably in the past. They lead traditional lives, but they are ready to embrace social and economic change – as long as they get a fair share of the benefits, and the chance to engage fully in the management of the changes. If Cambodia's resources were correctly managed, Cambodians as a whole could prosper. This is not happening at the moment. Local people are at a double disadvantage: first because a wealthy elite is taking the lion's share of the resources; and second because the central government is losing millions of dollars in unpaid tax revenue which could be spent on managing the forests and waterways, and building hospitals and schools in rural areas.

The government is largely responsible for what is happening and must act quickly to bring to an end the brutal rape of Cambodia's natural wealth. It is almost too late, but there is still time ... Our six families are waiting.

▲ *Buffalo and motorbike, Toeun village, Ratanakiri Province: rural people are not rooted unchangingly in the past.*

Jim Holmes

Urban poverty

From riches to rags

You are in east Phnom Penh, not far from the splendour of the Royal Palace. You are standing at the busy intersection of Preah Sihanouk Boulevard and Norodom Boulevard, the site of an impressive monument built in 1958 to commemorate Cambodia's independence from France. The Prime Minister's official residence is on one corner, flanked by a luxurious villa belonging to an international law firm. From the intersection you walk due east towards the Tonle Sap River. There are shops, bars, and smart restaurants along the wide tarmac street. Glance to your left and you may catch a glimpse of the five-star Cambodiana hotel overlooking the river and, next to the hotel, a floating casino, a popular location for tourists and wealthy Cambodians. In front of you is a fun fair, with Ferris wheel and sideshows, a mass of coloured lights, full of music and laughter after dark. Just before you reach the fair, you turn right off the wide boulevard and head down the narrower

Jim Holmes

▲ The Royal Palace (top), illuminated during the annual Water Festival in Phnom Penh – a world away from the squalor of nearby Bondos Vichea (right)

Samdech Sothearos Boulevard. Shops and restaurants give way to women crouching at the roadside selling vegetables, soup, and soft drinks. Children hawk chewing gum and cigarettes, worn-out cyclo drivers take a nap, young girls in ghostly white make-up sit nervously outside pink-lit brothels. There is an odour of decaying refuse.

You turn off Samdech Sothearos Boulevard and enter Bondos Vichea. You walk through a labyrinth of narrow, muddy streets between small, dark shacks, some made of wood, others of cardboard, packed together. There are people everywhere – children playing, men and women hurrying to and from work, street vendors haggling noisily with potential customers, a man on a bicycle trying to keep his balance in the throng. Turning off a street down a dark alleyway, no more than a metre wide, you come to the home of Kim Vanna, her husband, Chea Savou, and seven of their nine children. From the Independence Monument to here, you have travelled less than one kilometre.

▼ Kim Vanna with one of her nine children in their two-room shack in Bondos Vichea

Jim Holmes

The story of Vanna and Savou

Vanna and Savou came from Svay Rieng province to Phnom Penh in 1993 because they could not make a living from their small plot of land. When they first arrived in the city, they stayed at the Pro You Vong pagoda, courtesy of the Buddhist monks. Vanna and Savou erected a wooden house in the grounds of the pagoda, but found they did not have enough living space. So in 1995 they dismantled the house and came to Bondos Vichea, which is more central and offers a better opportunity to Savou, a barber, to make money.

One year after they moved in, the area was swept by a fire. It happened at night. No one knows whether the fire was an accident or an attempt to clear the residents from the area. Fortunately no one from Vanna's family was injured, though their house and few meagre belongings were destroyed. It took them a year to rebuild the house they live in now – a structure of thin, warped planks nailed crookedly around a precarious wooden frame, with two downstairs rooms and a mezzanine platform that serves as a third 'room'. The floor is mud. There are no running water or toilet facilities – the family uses an outside latrine or a plastic

Jim Holmes

bag, which is then tied up and thrown away. One bare electric bulb throws a weak light into the gloom. Apart from a wooden bed and some cooking pots, the family possesses no household items.

Vanna used to buy and sell empty cement bags to supplement her husband's earnings. Two years ago she had an abdominal operation which went wrong, and she finds she can no longer cope with physical work. They earn some extra money from renting out one of the downstairs rooms to two moto-taxi drivers; but, even with the rent, total earnings for the week come to only £10, which hardly pays for basic food, electricity, and water for the family. Fortunately Vanna has been able to borrow money from her brother to pay for medicine for Savou, who has tuberculosis, school fees for the one child they can afford to send to school, and some wood to mend the leaking roof. But her brother has problems of his own and is asking for the money back. She has no idea how to repay him.

'Our situation is hopeless,' says Vanna. 'We can't go back to Svay Rieng to farm, because there is not enough land; but we can't go on living like this. I need to find work to earn more money to support our children. Otherwise they will have no future.' She is trying. In 1997 she borrowed money from an organisation called the Urban Sector Group (USG) to start a small business. The idea was to buy and cook chickens and sell them on the street. She was just about to buy the chickens when fighting broke out on the outskirts of the city between armed forces loyal to Prince Ranariddh and those supporting Hun Sen. She decided that the lives of her children were more important than her business, so she left the city for a few days until the situation was calm. The money intended for the chickens was spent on food and shelter for the family. She has paid back the loan, but is cautious now about taking out another one.

Living on the edge

Bondos Vichea is home to 300 families – approximately 2000 people – living in an area no bigger than two football pitches. Like Vanna and Savou, the majority are rural people who, unable to eke out a living from the land, had no choice but to come to Phnom Penh to find work. The recent government census bears out the claims of urban-development groups that the number of poor Cambodians moving from the countryside to the cities is rising significantly. In Phnom Penh, alone, it is estimated that 20 per cent of the population of one million live below the poverty line in settlements such as Bondos Vichea, often in conditions of appalling squalor.

Because the urban poor have no political voice, their contribution to the economy tends to be overlooked. In fact, they play a vital role in Phnom Penh's development: they provide cheap, casual labour to the construction industry and factories; the moto-taxis and cyclo drivers are indispensable to the city's transport system; they offer a wide range of

▼ *Bondos Vichea: an area the size of two football pitches is home to 2000 people.*

Jim Holmes

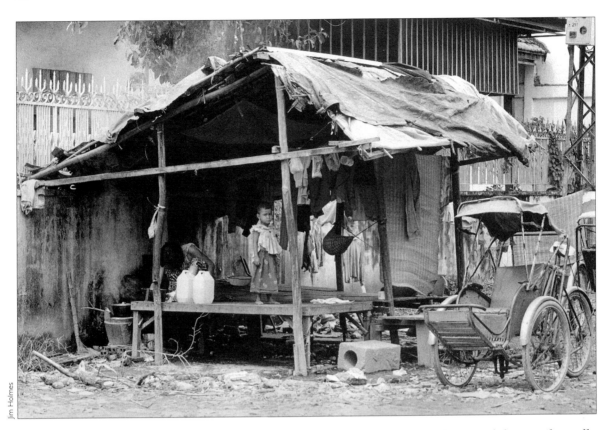

▲ *The one-room shack of a cyclo driver in Phnom Penh. One-fifth of the population of the capital city lives in extreme poverty.*

services, such as hairdressing, cleaning, and cooking; and they produce all kinds of food and drink to sell on the streets at reasonable prices. Cities need the poor, yet the poor remain on the edge of society, excluded from the wealth they help to create, without the most basic of services or land security. A recent survey by the Squatter and Urban Poor Federation (SUPF) showed that two-thirds of the urban poor are not served by toilets or piped water; two-thirds face regular flooding; one-third have been threatened with eviction; and one-fifth have experienced fires in their settlements.

The latest problem to confront the residents of Bondos Vichea is the threat of eviction. They happen to live on public land and have discovered that the government has sold it to a property developer, who plans to evict all the families. Residents have been told that they will be relocated to houses on a palm-oil plantation owned by a powerful businessman. The plantation is 150km away in the south of the country, near the port of Kompong Som; many residents have expressed a wish to stay in the city, but they fear that they will have no choice. They also doubt whether the businessman in question really will give them accommodation in return for working for him.

In Phnom Penh and other cities, people in similar situations are facing eviction as land values rise, and business people and politicians exploit the opportunity to get rich quick.

Self-help in the shanties

In 1994 men and women from Phnom Penh's poor settlements got together to form the SUPF. They argue from the premise that poor communities understand their own problems best and have the creative energy to solve those problems. Since then the SUPF and other organisations such as the USG have mobilised thousands of poor people to help themselves. Their schemes aim to make real improvements to people's lives at the lowest cost; they range from constructing community drainage systems to better housing, latrines, and roads.

Just as important as the material benefits, however, is the growing solidarity among the leaders and members of the various communities. On 13 July 1998, Seun Ratana, a ten-year-old boy, died by electrocution when he touched the gate of a school under construction in the Toul Svey Prey district of Phnom Penh. The local people demanded an apology and compensation from the contractor, who ignored them. Community leaders refused to give in, and more than one hundred of them joined forces and marched in protest to the Ministry of Justice, where they re-affirmed their demand to

▲ *A community sanitation project involving slum dwellers in Phnom Penh*

Jim Holmes

ministry officials. The contractor was subsequently ordered to pay compensation to the family. This was the first time that community leaders had acted together to protect the interests of one member, and their victory has given new heart to the entire urban poor population.

Sothea Phan is the USG community worker in Bondos Vichea. He recognises the changes that are going on among the urban poor. 'We are finding that people are supporting one another much more than before. We see this in our savings schemes, which are growing in popularity. People have enough trust to deposit money in the scheme. There is a committee elected by the community, which then decides how to allocate the loans. The system works well, because people know that if they don't pay back a loan or pay in their deposits, they will be letting others down. And they also realise that access to credit to start small business ventures is the only way for people to improve their lives.' Speaking of the threat of eviction by the government, Phan is realistic: 'We are up against a powerful force, but we will talk to the government and try to reach a solution. The government must understand that the poor have a voice and must be listened to. People have come to Bondos Vichea for a reason. It is unfair to assume that they will automatically want to go elsewhere. They have rights like anyone else, and they must be respected.'

Before the 1998 elections, urban community leaders delivered their demands to the politicians in the form of a statement which they asked the political parties to sign:

- The government must recognise our right to live where we live now. Give us the assurance that we will not be evicted.

- If the government needs the land where we live, then we must be relocated to a site of our choosing, close to job opportunities, with basic infrastructure like water, sanitation, and roads.

- The government must guarantee us access to clean drinking water.

- The government must support us in getting a sanitation system for our settlement.

- An amount must be set aside in the municipal budget for the improvement of urban poor settlements.

- The government must do all in its power to create job opportunities and not harass us in the market or work place.

- Development in favour of the poor must be the government's topmost priority.

▼ Sary, one of 20,000 children who live and work on the streets of Phnom Penh, collects rubbish to sort and sell.

Jim Holmes

Vanna wants to stay in Bondos Vichea. 'If we knew that we would not be moved out, we would invest more in our house and our community. I would go out to work to earn money; but, as it is, we are on the edge, with nowhere to go. Why can't the government understand that and help us?'

The street child

Sary is 14 and has been living on the street for three years with his mother and brother. He and his brother work as beggars around the central market. Individually they earn the equivalent of 40 pence a day, some of which they have to give to older street children to avoid a beating. When he is not begging, Sary spends his time sorting through piles of rubbish. His mother sells vegetables in the market, and at night the three sleep together on the pavement nearby. The family came to Phnom Penh in 1991 from Poipet, on the Thai–Cambodian border. The family had lived in a refugee camp throughout the 1980s, but Sary's father did not want to go back to being a poor farmer, so he took a job in a sawmill in the city. Soon after arriving, he left his wife for another woman. Sary's mother was unable to keep paying the rent on a small house, and the family was forced on to the street. Sary did not want to stay with his father, because of the violent beatings he used to get.

'Life on the street is difficult,' he says. 'I'm cold at night, because I don't have a blanket or a mosquito net. I've never been to school, because my mother can't afford to send me, though I would love to learn to read and write and go on to study. I never get enough to eat and I depend on handouts of food from the foodstall owners.'

An estimated 20,000 children now live on the streets of Phnom Penh, double the number quoted in a 1995 UNICEF report. Several local and international NGOs are working with street children, but their efforts are being swamped by the scale of the problem. Much more must be done to understand and help street children. They are not only being denied a decent childhood, but are also increasingly at risk of sexual exploitation in a country where the small and the weak are prey to roving pimps and brothel owners. What will the future be like for children like Sary, and what will they be able to offer the future?

▼ *Working on the streets of Phnom Penh, young waste-pickers risk exploitation and abuse.*

Jim Holmes

Women's lives

▲ *Sey Samon and her children at 'home': a wooden bed covered in plastic sheeting on a muddy river bank in Phnom Penh*

Samon's story

Samon was born in 1965 in a small village in Prey Veng province, some 60km east of Phnom Penh. Her parents were rice farmers. She was the youngest of six children, three boys and three girls. She remembers her childhood as a happy time – until the Khmer Rouge seized power in 1975. She went to the local primary school from the age of six until the school closed in the same year; then she spent much of her time helping her mother with household chores and looking after chickens. Her sisters tended a small vegetable garden, and she remembers all the family working to plant and harvest the rice.

While thousands of Cambodians fled to Thailand following the Vietnamese invasion in 1979, Samon's family stayed. She wanted to continue her education and go on to secondary school like her elder brothers, but she was not allowed to. Instead, she was given the task of growing and selling vegetables in the local market. As a result she is almost illiterate.

Samon married Prak Ol in 1988. As is customary, they moved into a house in her village, close to her parents, and began growing rice on a small plot allocated to them by the village leader. By 1991 Samon and Ol had two children. The marriage was relatively happy, despite the continual struggle to make a living. They shared the farm work, but Samon was left to tend their vegetable garden, raise chickens, do the washing, cleaning, and cooking, and bring up their son and daughter.

By 1993 the couple were finding it increasingly hard to make ends meet, so they decided to go to Phnom Penh during the dry season to earn extra money. They found work as casual labourers at a cement factory, loading 50kg bags of cement on to lorries. Soon after they arrived, Ol began an affair with a woman from the same village in Prey Veng, and began beating up his wife. The beatings went on in the room that they shared with other families. They saw what was going on, but no one intervened. Ol left Samon in Phnom Penh, but later went back to her. She took him in and became pregnant again. Three months later, Ol gave her the most savage beating yet and then left. Samon has not seen him since.

The beating left her with serious internal injuries, but she could not afford medical treatment, and continued carrying bags of cement. She had no choice: her two children needed feeding and clothing. After six months of pain and bleeding she collapsed and was taken to hospital. The child in her womb had died. Samon spent time afterwards in a women's hostel with her children, recovering from the operation. Sadly, her story is not uncommon in Cambodia today.

The mainstay of Cambodian society

In 1979, after a decade of civil war and genocide, it was left mainly to women to pick up the pieces and rebuild society. Men had died in greater numbers, and women made up two-thirds of the adult population.

The women of Cambodia responded to the challenge, despite the demographic imbalance, which made finding a husband more difficult, and the trauma of losing members of their families, which left deep psychological scars. In the fledgling People's Republic of Kampuchea (PRK) women found jobs in factories, making up two-thirds of the workforce in State-run industries; they filled one-third of the posts in the civil service; and began to participate in the running of central and local government. In the 1988 National Assembly one-fifth of members were women, and in the 1980s one woman held the rank of minister, two were vice-ministers, and others became department heads. Within the ruling Communist Party, one-sixth of the members of the central committee were women. There was one female provincial governor and a number of women with posts at district and commune level. Equal rights, based on the UN charter for human rights, were enshrined in the 1989 constitution.

Responsibility for feeding a malnourished population lay with the rural population, the bulk of whom were now women. When those who had been displaced returned to their home villages, they had to contend with tasks such as ploughing and harrowing, which had traditionally been carried out by men. They were helped by the formation of *krom samaki*, or solidarity groups, a form of communal labour whereby plots of land assigned to individuals were farmed by the group. Though the system was unpopular among many Cambodians because of its echoes of life under the Khmer Rouge, the *krom samaki* did benefit women and old people, unable to manage on their own.

Jim Holmes

Women became group leaders and deputies. When the business of selling food and other products in the markets resumed, some 85 per cent of the market-trade workforce consisted of women. They had no choice: their children required feeding and clothing.

Education and health services, systematically destroyed by the Khmer Rouge, remained limited, especially for women, throughout the 1980s. The economic blockade imposed on the PRK by the USA, China, and a number of western European governments compounded the nation's problems. Nevertheless, women responded to the call to replenish the depleted population, in spite of high mortality rates among mothers and children. And girls and young women went back to school. Although enrolment levels for secondary and higher education declined after primary-school years, by 1989 one-quarter of students at Phnom Penh University were women.

Losing ground in the 1990s

The story of the next decade was different. As the twentieth century drew to a close, women continued to make up the majority of the workforce in both the formal and informal sectors of the economy, yet their representation in decision-making at all levels of society declined. The 1993 elections, apparently heralding the return to democracy for Cambodia, saw only seven women elected, out of 120 members of the National Assembly, compared with one-fifth in 1988; women fared slightly better in the 1998 elections, when 12 women entered the National Assembly, two becoming ministers. At the local level, especially in rural areas, women remain grossly under-represented: none of the provincial governors is a woman; a 1994 study by the Secretariat for Women's Affairs noted that, while the return of men reduced the labour burden on rural women, 'women are partly losing control over rice cultivation as their access to irrigation tools is hindered, and their participation in irrigation ... is reduced because they are discouraged from participating in decision-making processes.' Out

▼ *Women run the markets and do much of the agricultural work in Cambodia.*

Jim Holmes

of a total of 3600 commune leaders, fewer than ten are women. Anecdotal evidence points to a disproportionate increase in the number of landless women.

In general the introduction of a free market has not helped women. As government factories were closed down or privatised, the majority of those workers laid off were women. And with the changeover came the closure of nearly all the 80 or so child-care centres provided by the socialist State. The downsizing of the civil service as part of the World Bank stabilisation package, aimed at 'rescuing' Cambodia's ailing economy, has led to the laying off of thousands of employees, most of whom are women. They have had no choice but to take badly paid jobs in privately owned factories and in the burgeoning service sector, which includes the sex industry. It is estimated that women earn less than half the amount that their male counterparts are paid for most occupations, and involvement in the sex trade carries with it the ever higher risk of HIV infection, Cambodia's new killer.

Fighting discrimination

Samon was fortunate to have her hospital bill paid by Khemara, one of a growing number of non-government organisations (NGOs) dedicated to supporting women and improving their rights. Khemara, the first Cambodian NGO to be founded in 1991 (with the help of Oxfam), also runs the hostel where Samon and her children first stayed after the operation. Samon's experiences of domestic violence are not isolated. Khemara estimates that one-third of the women who are assisted by its range of programmes are physically abused by husbands and partners. Nationwide the figure is put at one-fifth.

Domestic violence is symptomatic of the discrimination against women in society. The causes lie in a deep-rooted prejudice, expressed in the traditional values of the *Chbab Srey* – an attitude that continues to deny women their basics rights to education, health care, decent pay and work conditions, and security.

Khemara and others are working to counter discrimination. Lev Bunna, its programme officer in charge of the family-support service, explains the strategy: 'In the long term we have to challenge and change attitudes that society holds about women. This means getting women to value the work they do, whether it be as housewife, mother, or employee, in order to raise their self-esteem. We also need to convince men that women have the same rights as they do and

... never turn your back to your husband when he sleeps and never touch his head without first bowing in his honour ... respect and fear the wishes of your husband and take his advice to heart ... if your husband gives an order, don't hesitate a moment in responding ... avoid posing yourself as equal to your husband, who is your master; if he insults you, go to your room and reflect, never insult or talk back to him ... have patience, prove your patience, never responding to his excessive anger ... but use gentle language in response.

Extract from the *Chbab Srey* ('Rules of the Lady')

Like most Cambodian women, Sey Samon is familiar with the *Chbab Srey* verse. As a young girl, her grandmother, mother, and teacher drummed the lines into her. Samon, by contrast, never mentions the verse to her daughter. She would like her to learn a different set of values.

SOLD FOR £175

Men Kim Loth, aged 23, looks like any ordinary, bright, young woman as she sits weaving at the loom. Her past has been anything but ordinary, however. She comes from a poor farming family in Svay Rieng province. Two years ago a woman called at her parents' house and told them that a family in Phnom Penh needed a maid to take care of the house and cook. In return, the maid would earn 30,000 Riels a month (£8), which was more than her father earned. Loth accepted the offer and went to Phnom Penh. There she was tricked by the owner of the house into going to Battambang to see a relative, and was sold to a brothel for £175. She was a prisoner for seven months, forced to work as a prostitute every day, from seven in the morning until one o'clock the following morning, in order to repay her 'debt' to the brothel keeper. Some men, not all, used condoms. She was given no money. Food depended on her popularity with the customers: the more men she attracted, the better the food; conversely, few customers meant hardly anything to eat.

At the end of seven months Loth was spotted by a former teacher, who contacted her father. She was released by the police, after her father had paid them off. Taken back to Phnom Penh, she lived with an aunt, but soon afterwards she fell ill and developed fever. She was diagnosed as HIV-positive. 'I wanted to die,' she says, 'but I was fortunate to make contact with the Cambodian Women's Development Agency (CWDA), which has helped me to get my life back together. I have learned how to weave and, more importantly, I am now a trained counsellor, helping others to come to terms with HIV/AIDS. I tell them that life can be good.' Loth does not have many plans for the future, but would love to progress within the CWDA and become its director one day. 'I'd like to help women who have been victims of exploitation, as well as widows and disabled women.'

▲ *'We need to convince men that women have the same rights as they do, and do equally valuable work.'*

do equally valuable work.' But groups like Khemara know that changing attitudes is not enough. Women need the opportunity to improve the quality of their lives and their children's. They therefore run literacy and numeracy classes for women, and make education available for children who have dropped out of school. Khemara offers health care, crucial to women's well-being in a country where the maternal mortality rate is the highest in Asia. It provides training in catering and other skills, and offers loans to women who want to use their skills to start small businesses – an all-round package to give women like Samon a fair chance.

Women's NGOs also recognise the importance of lobbying the male-dominated government to introduce legislation to protect women's rights. Thanks to their efforts, important legislation has been passed: in 1997 new laws on trafficking, domestic violence, and abortions were ratified, and the Labour Code of 1997 offers special protection to working women.

There is clearly a long way to go before legislation is fully respected by those who apply it. Only when women are fully represented, not only at all levels of government but also in institutions such as the judicial system and the media, can this become reality. Meanwhile, women like Samon will carry on doing the very best they can for themselves and their children. 'I have to look forward now,' she says. 'I've found a place to stay down by the river. It's a wooden bed with plastic sheeting for a roof, but it will be home until I can find something better.' She will go back to the cement factory in the short term, but will take advantage of Khemara's training schemes and try to start a small business, possibly selling cakes: 'I will be fine on my own. I don't need men. I could never trust them again.'

Living with landmines

Jim Holmes

▲ *Mong Bora, who lost his left leg in a landmine explosion in the forest near his house*

Imagine that whenever you leave the house you have to be careful where you tread. Imagine that every time you dig the garden to plant flowers and vegetables, it may prove fatal. Imagine, as a parent, no matter how many times you have warned the children, you worry that every time they go off to play they might be maimed or killed. And imagine having no choice but to live in constant fear.

This is not imagination, but reality for Mong Bora, his wife, Mot Savate, and their two young sons, who live in Chisang village – a village in a minefield, surrounded by mined farmland and mined forest.

The story of Bora and Savate

Bora was born in Chisang in 1944. The village is in Rattanak Mondol ('Mountain of Gems'), a district of Battambang Province. The soil is dark and rich, some of the most fertile in Cambodia, supporting the staple rice crop as well as cotton, peanuts, oranges, and a variety of vegetables. The flat land around Chisang, in the central part of the district, verges on tree-covered highlands in the west, where the gemstones are to be found. Rounded limestone hillocks and palm trees protrude above the plains, breaking the monotony of the skyline. To the south are the waters of the Sangke river, muddied by gem prospecting.

Bora has lived in the village all his life, except when he and his wife were forced to escape from fighting in 1989 and again in 1994. They came back in 1995, determined to stay, and were allocated a small plot of land, measuring only one-tenth of a hectare, on which to build a house. They have another plot of just under half a hectare close to the village pagoda, which was destroyed by the Khmer Rouge in 1989. 'Chisang is my home,' explains Bora. 'My parents and grandparents lived here, and I want to spend my life here. I belong here.' Even though his house and field are in a marked minefield, and even though he lost a leg to a landmine in 1992?

The accident is still vivid in his memory. 'I was with other people from the village, collecting rattan from the forest, about two kilometres away from here. It was the dry season and we were going to sell the rattan in the local town. I was some way from the others when I heard a terrific explosion. I saw them stop and look at me. For a moment I didn't know what had happened. I didn't feel any pain, only a sense of calm. Then I looked down and realised what had happened. My right foot wasn't there, just blood, bits of flesh, the leg-bone sticking out. I shouted, tried to move, but fell over and then excruciating pain hit me. I passed out. My friends carried me to Sdao hospital, and on the way I was given first aid by a UN team. From there I was taken to the provincial hospital in Battambang.'

Bora had stepped on a blast mine, probably a Chinese Type 72, which is designed not to kill but to tear off a foot or lower leg in a single, explosive blast. The other type of landmine is the fragmentation mine, planted above ground and detonated by a trip wire, expelling ball bearings or shards of metal, which kill at close range and are able to rip through flesh at distances up to 500m. In war, landmines provide a cost-effective way to demoralise an advancing force, which must use up time and resources to care for the victims, rather than being able to leave corpses behind and move on. In peace time, landmines go on injuring and killing. They do not discriminate between soldier and child. They are the perfect weapon for guerrilla forces which lack the numbers to capture and hold on to territory. Landmines are their silent, ever wakeful sentinels, their weapon of choice.

Bora recovered after a long and expensive stay in hospital – financed by money from a loan shark. He was fitted with a prosthesis at a rehabilitation centre run by the International Committee of the Red Cross. It allows him to walk and work, although his stump is sometimes painful, and he cannot walk very far. He has to rely for many things on his wife, which bothers him at times.

Shortage of arable land is the main problem for the family. There is land available in the area, but most of it is thought to be mined, so it lies fallow, within sight of poor villagers, who desperately need it. Bora has been tempted, but will not risk ploughing up a new plot. He cannot afford to lose his other leg, and he has seen too many villagers maimed. This year, however, he was forced to plough up the land beside the house for the first time. He thought it would be safe. He found two blast mines buried there. There are mines and unexploded bombs everywhere in Rattanak Mondol. How did they get there?

From prosperity to poverty – Rattanak Mondol's legacy of conflict

Chisang lies on Route 10, the main road between Battambang and Pailin, to the west of the towns of Sdao and Treng. Until the late 1980s, the area was prosperous. The towns supported a population of 10,000, had electricity, paved roads, pagodas, and concrete houses. Then in September

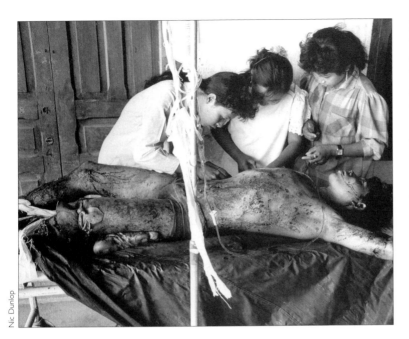

▲ *Nearly 50,000 Cambodians injured by landmines have undergone amputations; many more die without receiving medical attention.*

1989, the Vietnamese began their final withdrawal from Cambodia as part of the UN-brokered peace plan. This was what the Khmer Rouge had been waiting for. They flooded eastwards over the Thai border back into Cambodia. The Cambodian army's response to the advancing guerrilla force was to lay mines, which it had in plentiful supply. Both sides of Route 10, as well as the edges of forests and valleys, were mined in an attempt to contain the Khmer Rouge advance. The strategy failed.

The Cambodian army did manage to halt the advance in late 1990 and then proceeded to go on the offensive, pushing the Khmer Rouge back whence they had come. The latter laid yet more mines and booby traps as they retreated. Rather than using them as a purely defensive weapon, however, the Khmer Rouge buried them in fields, in irrigation channels, around wells, and, sometimes, near schools and hospitals in a deliberate attempt not only to kill and maim civilians but also to demoralise them and destroy their livelihoods. The tactic proved successful and very cheap to implement. A blast mine costs as little as £2. The potential damage it can cause is inestimable.

By the summer of 1991, an uneasy peace had returned to the area. Chisang found itself on Rattanak Mondol's front line, caught between government troops and the Khmer Rouge. More mines were laid by the Cambodian Army, wary of the guerrillas who had established their base in Pailin. Heavy fighting broke out again in 1994, as first the renamed Royal Cambodian Armed Forces (RCAF) and then the Khmer Rouge made pushes into each other's territory. In May of that year Bora and his family, along with most of the population of Rattanak Mondol, were, once more, living as refugees in Battambang.

Now Treng town is largely uninhabited; Sdao's buildings still bear the scars of the thousands of shells that hit it; large swathes of fertile land cannot be cultivated; and in Chisang, one in ten families has an amputee member, usually the adult male.

The price to be paid by the poor

Because of past conflict, Rattanak Mondol is probably Cambodia's most densely mined district – more often than not, it tops the mine-casualty lists – but just how many mines there are in the area and in the rest of

Cambodia is unclear. Estimates for the country range from 500,000 to six million, making Cambodia one of the most heavily mined countries in the world. Added to the mines are the hundreds of thousands of unexploded shells, rockets, and bombs that litter the countryside. The US airforce alone dropped half a million tons of ordnance in the early 1970s, the remains of which are still killing and maiming people today.

It is estimated that up to 3000 sq km of land, much of it prime agricultural land or forest, is contaminated by landmines and cannot be used, or is being used at the cost of Cambodian lives and limbs. And what a price innocent Cambodians are paying. Until Former Yugoslavia erupted in violence, Cambodia had the dubious distinction of having the greatest number of amputees per head of population – 46,000, the size of a small town, or one in 236, compared with one in 22,000 in the USA. Numbers of victims killed by landmines are more difficult to predict. In 1998, approximately 20 per cent of mine victims died from their injuries, but it is assumed that many more die, mainly small children and women, without becoming statistics. Of the amputees, 90 per cent are men, aged mostly between 22 and 35: soldiers and farmers, fathers and husbands, mainly poor, in the prime of their adult lives. With a leg missing, they cannot work as well as they did, which imposes an added burden on the rest of the family, in terms of extra work to be done and extra money needed to pay hospital bills. And for poor families, unexpected bills mean falling further into debt.

The loss of a limb leaves deep psychological scars: amputee men often feel inadequate and vent their frustration by beating their wives; amputee women are almost always abandoned by their husbands; and amputee men and women may find themselves rejected by a society imbued with the Buddhist concept of 'wholeness of body': amputees, significantly, are excluded from religious orders. Many end up as beggars, still wearing their tattered military uniforms.

The litany of devastation is never ending. The presence of landmines and bombs is a major cause of poverty and represents the most serious obstacle to Cambodia's development.

Nic Dunlop

▲ *The price of an anti-personnel mine is $3; the true cost is the shattered life of an innocent civilian.*

Cleaning up the pollution

The only way to make mined areas safe for people to live and work in is to remove all the mines from the ground. To date there is no quick fix to the problem; but there is a long-term solution: it lies in mobilising people and training them to locate the mines, using metal detectors. The work is slow, expensive, and dangerous, but Cambodians are tackling the enormous task with great energy. Leading the way is the Cambodian Mine Action Centre (CMAC), although its reputation has been tarnished by allegations of high-level corruption. CMAC is ably assisted by international de-mining agencies, mostly staffed by Cambodians, trained by ex-patriate explosives experts.

Together they have cleared only a small proportion of the estimated number of landmines, but, by careful targeting of mined land needed for housing and agriculture, or mined areas blocking access to schools and clinics, these organisations are making a real difference to the lives of large numbers of people. Declining injury rates prove it. Chisang is currently being de-mined by the Mines Advisory Group (MAG), a British-based organisation. The suspected areas have been marked off, and paths through the village have been cleared. The area around the village well, long since abandoned, will be cleared next, saving people a 15-minute walk.

▲ *Sok Cheuon, a fisherman in Kandal village, lost his left leg to a landmine.*

It will take MAG's Cambodian de-miners, male and female, many months to make Chisang and its surrounding lands safe, but already Bora and Savate are feeling more secure, especially when it comes to letting their children out to play. The de-mining agencies could easily mobilise more clearance teams, if only they had more funds.

A small step towards ridding the world of landmines was taken in December 1997 with the signing of the Ottawa Treaty, which bans the sale and use of landmines. More than one hundred countries, including Cambodia, signed it, and enough have now ratified it to make it a legal obligation for all signatories to destroy their stocks and stop using this insidious weapon. The treaty's teeth remain blunt, however, because China, Russia, and the USA refused to sign. They are among the largest producers of landmines. While the treaty will do nothing to solve Cambodia's immediate difficulties, it was hoped that governments would be encouraged to invest significantly more resources in clearing the mines in the ground. Unfortunately nothing has happened yet. The de-mining agencies, and Bora and his wife, are still waiting ...

A ban will do little to change the mind-set of Cambodians, who have grown accustomed to using landmines in their everyday lives, despite knowing the damage they can cause. Bora admits that it is common to find a fisherman or hunter chipping the explosive from inside a plastic mine, to which is attached a detonator, in order to kill fish and animals. People use mines at night to protect their property, storing them in the house during the day, where they are occasionally found and detonated by unsuspecting children. And it is not unusual to find shell casings still containing explosive in blacksmiths' workshops.

Meanwhile, Bora and Savate carry on working. It is harvest time and they are about to gather in the rice crop from the plot beside the house where Bora found the mines. Bora is unhappy about using this land, knowing that he almost stood on another mine. But he admits, 'When hunger bites, you will do almost anything and take whatever risks are necessary to survive.'

Health care and education: empty promises?

*The State shall ... guarantee the principles of educational freedom
and equality to ensure that all citizens have an equal opportunity to
earn a living.* (Article 65 of the 1993 Cambodian Constitution)

*The health of the people shall be guaranteed ... Poor citizens shall
receive free medical consultation.*
(Article 72 of the 1993 Cambodian Constitution)

These are bold promises from the government of one of the world's
poorest countries, made after more than two decades of civil war, which
saw the ranks of doctors and teachers decimated. But are the promises
being kept? Are the health and education of all Cambodians – men,
women, and children – being guaranteed?

Tep Seng and Kim Sopheap, our Kreung tribespeople from
Ratankiri, do not think the government is honouring its promises. 'The
nearest hospital is in Banlung, 30km away. As there is no public transport,
we normally walk, and that takes us about five hours. Because the hospital
is always crowded, we usually have to stay two or three days before seeing a
doctor. Treatment isn't free, either. The consultation and medicine may
cost up to 18,000 Riels (£3), which is expensive, when your annual income

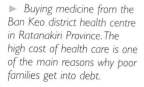

► *Buying medicine from the
Ban Keo district health centre
in Ratanakiri Province. The
high cost of health care is one
of the main reasons why poor
families get into debt.*

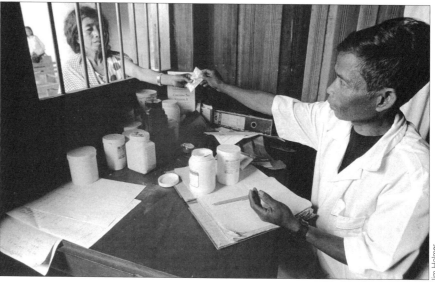

Jim Holmes

is no more than 180,000 Riels (£30). Then there are the costs of accommodation and food during our stay in the town. And, of course, we are losing valuable work-time while we are away.' There is a small clinic at Kambak village, two kilometres away, but the service isn't good. Seng says that the health workers are not properly trained, nor are there adequate supplies of medicine. For most ailments, the family has to rely on traditional medicine.

Chhoun Yeath in Battambang rarely uses the government health services either, preferring to pay for a private nurse in the village whenever her children are sick. The nurse is expensive, but Yeath trusts him. She's less careful about her own health, though, because she can't afford treatment for herself. Her children always come first.

Chea Rith and Chenda Mach in Kompong Chnnang find it difficult to afford any kind of health care. They rely on a local pharmacist to diagnose illnesses and prescribe drugs. They know they are taking a risk, because the pharmacist has no medical training and because the drugs he prescribes may be past their sell-by date, but poverty gives them no choice.

In Phnom Penh, health facilities are more easily available, even for the poor. On average, 80 per cent of people in towns are within reach of some sort of health facility, in contrast to only 50 per cent of rural people. Yeath and the Kreung family are quite fortunate to be close to a clinic, even though the service is poor. Kim Vanna and her husband, Chea Savou, living in Bondos Vichea, are within easy reach of the Kuntha Bopha clinic in Phnom Penh, which is funded by Swiss aid money and is, consequently, well staffed and equipped. They pay nothing for consultations and very little for medicine. Without this lifeline, Vanna does not know how the family would survive. 'Ordinary government facilities aren't good in Phnom Penh, especially when it comes to dealing with women's health. I preferred to go to a private hospital for an operation after the birth of my last child, rather than take the risk of something going wrong in a State hospital, even though it cost us our entire savings.' The operation, performed at a Chinese-run hospital at a cost of £40, still went wrong.

The education system draws a slightly more positive response. 'Education is the only way to make your life better,' says Yeath. She would love at least one of her children to become a teacher. Other parents agree, and all of them, except one, live within walking distance of a primary school. They would like all their children to attend, but, as with health care, cost is the prohibiting factor. Vanna has six children of school age, but can afford to educate only her 13-year-old son. Neither she, her husband, nor any one of her other children can read or write. Registration fees for the year may be only 3000 Riels (70 pence), but there is additional expenditure for uniforms, books, pencils, paper, food, and sometimes transport. A poor household may spend up to one-tenth of its income on educating one child at primary school.

Despite the costs, Cambodians somehow manage to enrol three-quarters of their children in primary school; but only a quarter of that

Jim Holmes

▲ *One quarter of all Cambodian children are excluded from the education system. This boy's family cannot afford a uniform for him.*

number enter secondary school, and only a small proportion of those are girls. If access to health care in Cambodia is determined by where you live, then access to education, especially secondary and higher education, depends largely on your sex. It is probably no coincidence that Vanna and Savou have decided to educate a son rather than a daughter. The traditional attitude to young unmarried women is that they should not stray far from home – secondary schools are mainly located in towns – where they should look after siblings and learn how to be housewives, rather than getting an education in preparation for paid employment. Reality shows that this view is hopelessly outdated, and that more and more women are choosing to find jobs, most often out of necessity.

Poor health

Sey Samon understands the serious consequences of being excluded from both education and health care. 'I was in desperate need of help after my husband beat me up. He kicked me in the stomach when I was pregnant, and I was bleeding badly. But I simply did not have the money to get to the hospital, let alone pay to see a doctor and get treatment.' She knows that she has seriously jeopardised her own health and any possibility of having another child. If she cannot work, who will provide for her children? Who will send them to school? And if they are denied a good start in life, including a basic education, they will find themselves in the same poverty trap that has ensnared their mother.

The others know how unsatisfactory health care can affect their lives and their livelihoods: Vanna's botched operation means that she can no longer contribute to the family income; and her husband, Savou, who is now the main breadwinner and needs to work longer hours, cannot do so because he has tuberculosis, the result of poor nutrition and hygiene. Seng and Sopheap in Ratanakiri have lost two children, one following heavy bleeding through the mouth, the other to a fever and weight loss. They took both to hospital repeatedly, but were sent away each time after being told that nothing could be done; they still do not know why their children died. Men Kim Loth's life has been radically altered after learning that she is HIV-positive. Ministry of Health testing suggests that at least 100,000 Cambodians are already HIV-positive, among them a very high proportion of female sex workers. If major steps are not taken to counter the spread of the disease, it is predicted that 500,000 – almost one in 20 of the population – will be infected by the year 2006.

Malaria, tuberculosis, diarrhoea, and fevers are all too common: the price to be paid not only for unsatisfactory health care, but also for the lack of clean water and safe sanitation. High costs of health care, coupled with the inferior quality of the care on offer, are affecting all poor Cambodians, but statistics show that women are being disproportionately affected. A World Health Organisation report showed that Cambodian women are 44 times more likely to die from a malarial infection than men, because their general health and nutritional status are poorer. Just as serious is the maternal mortality rate in Cambodia: estimated at 900 deaths per 100,000 live births, one of the highest in the world, it is due not only to a lack of midwifery skills, but also to the intense pressure on married women to have children from early on in marriage into their forties.

▶ *Health education on the streets of Phnom Penh: the government is making an effort to promote contraception and safe sex.*

Jim Holmes

Poor education

There are strong links between education and health – and they are especially important when it comes to women's education. Studies have shown that educating women improves their own health and that of their children; and that educated women are, in turn, more likely to educate their daughters. However, in Cambodia access to education for women, at primary and secondary levels, is seriously inadequate, as is health education about contraception.

With large numbers of the population excluded from the education system, and high rates of drop-out and repetition, Cambodia has one of the lowest figures for adult literacy in south-east Asia. The United Nations Development Programme estimates it at only one-third of the population, a proportion that corresponds to the rate of poverty (although one-fifth of prosperous Cambodian women are also illiterate). Most members of our six families, parents included, cannot read and write and are aware how their lack of education has severely restricted opportunities to make a better life for themselves and their families. The fundamental disadvantage of illiteracy is that it limits people's job prospects. The employment market is expanding in Cambodia: jobs are on offer with national and foreign companies, but well-paid positions in the private sector and stable careers in the government demand the ability to read and write – and usually much more. Without a basic education, the potential of large numbers of people remains untapped: they are condemned to poorly paid, unfulfilling work, and the economy of Cambodia suffers incalculably.

▼ Education offers a way out of poverty, but girls are still at a disadvantage when it comes to secondary and higher education.

Jim Holmes

Even if they find work, illiterate people cannot read about their rights, and are more likely to be exploited by employers. Illiterate women, already suffering discrimination because of their sex, are at a particular disadvantage, earning, on average, 50 per cent less than their male colleagues. And in rural areas, farmers like Yeath and the other members of her VDC risk losing their land, because they do not have written titles for their plots, failing to see the importance of something they cannot understand, and unaware of current legislation and how they can use it to protect their interests. Yeath recognises her vulnerability, but remains complacent in the belief that her plot is not at risk.

Providing health care and education

In 1979 the last of the Khmer Rouge fled to Thailand, leaving a nation to come to terms with the deaths of more than one-seventh of the population, and the systematic destruction of its economic and social fabric. The Khmer Rouge had targeted educated Cambodians, in particular, considering them a threat to Cambodia's new-found 'egalitarianism'. Out of 500 doctors, 50 remained alive in 1979; 15,000 teachers met their deaths, and only 5000 survived. Schools, hospitals, and clinics were abandoned; books, government records, and equipment were deliberately destroyed.

The new Vietnamese-backed government had the task of rebuilding the health and education services almost from scratch, without external loans or aid, denied to them by China and the West. Since then, successive Cambodian governments would argue that much has been achieved under difficult circumstances to bring health care and education to the people, though they would also have to admit that there is a long way to go before the pledges in the constitution are met.

Lack of political will on the part of the government to make funding available for health and education is the main problem. Only five per cent of the budget (about £1 per head each year) is spent on health care and ten per cent on education, compared with more than 50 per cent spent on defence. A significant proportion of both health and education expenditure is provided by international donors. Much of the budgets, however, is consumed by administration costs, leaving a shortfall in funds for decent staff salaries and training, equipment, and essential medicine.

Ban Keo district health centre illustrates the funding problem. Situated 30km east of Banlung in Ratanakiri, the clinic serves a population of 12,000 people. Attendance is low, because a significant section of the population lives too far away to use the clinic regularly, if at all. The centre has a vaccination service, two midwives, a laboratory, and four general health assistants. This clinic benefits from support by Health Unlimited (HU), a British agency, which provides stocks of essential drugs, vaccines, and medical equipment; but some patients complain about the service, according to a spokesperson of HU: 'The real problem is the level of

Jim Holmes

▲ Vaccination programmes for children and adults suffer from shortage of funds. The government spends only £1 per capita on health care each year.

salaries paid to the staff by the government,' he explains. 'They are very low and are often paid two or three months late. Staff are also ill-trained. The midwife, for example, received only two months' training in Banlung medical school. This means that staff are not motivated and can't afford to spend the necessary hours at the clinic, because they need to work elsewhere to feed their families. Consequently, vital personnel are not present when they should be, and local people become disillusioned with the service and stop coming.'

Thon Sita, Director of Preah Chdao primary school in Battambang, is standing in the library. The walls are made of the wood from empty Russian bullet boxes. The roof is made of rusting sheets of corrugated iron. Well-thumbed books are stacked up on a single table. There are no chairs. Like the clinic staff in Ban Keo, Thon Sita is unhappy about the situation. 'We need cupboards for these books, otherwise they get eaten by insects, and we can't afford to replace them. We also need to rebuild some classrooms and build others, because the numbers of children wanting to come to the school are growing. We need typewriters, and chairs for staff and children. So many things, but we don't have the money.' And salaries? 'The quality of teaching since I entered the profession ten years ago has not improved, because teachers are simply not paid enough to live on. Poverty among teachers is the main reason for poor-quality education in Cambodia.'

The school has received some help from UNICEF and other organisations, but what encourages Thon Sita more than anything else is the support given by local people. 'We have an effective parent–teacher association in Preah Chdao. Business people who send their children here have been very generous, making cash donations towards equipment and repairs. And poorer parents also contribute by offering their labour to build classrooms and carry out repairs. We get help from a local theatre group which raises money for us. Without their help, we would find it very difficult to continue.' Over half the schools in Cambodia have a parent–teacher association.

In the run-up to the 1998 elections, the two main political parties used promises of education to woo the voters. School buildings began to spring up in remote villages, paid for by the parties. However, with insufficient government money to staff or equip them, the buildings will probably remain empty.

▼ Preah Chdao Primary School in Battambang Province depends on parents to build classrooms and do repairs.

Jim Holmes

Self-reliance in the face of empty promises

Instead of relying upon politicians, local people and organisations are making their own provision for health care and education, often supported by international agencies. The Cambodian Women's Development Association, Khemara, Non-Timber Forest Products, and Aphivat Strey, which supports the VDC of which Yeath is a member, all run literacy classes, and some have established clinics. Services are not normally free, but experience has shown that poor people are prepared to pay in cash or in kind – by offering their labour, for example – if they believe that they are benefiting. The notion that the poor rely on handouts is wrong.

Poor health care and limited education are among the main causes of poverty. The rights to health and education are enshrined in the Cambodian constitution, and the government repeatedly pledges to increase expenditure on these two essential services. But promises are being broken, and trust is being lost. Cambodian organisations are doing their best to respond to the unmet needs, but resources at their disposal are limited. Without genuine commitment from the Cambodian government, its citizens will go on dying in ignorance.

Breaking the cycle of violence and mistrust

'Hatred never ceases by hatred. Violence never ceases by violence. This is an eternal truth.'
(The Buddha)

Fifteen kilometres south-west of Phnom Penh is Choeung Ek ('The Killing Fields'). Twenty thousand men, women and children, innocent victims of a paranoid regime, were taken here from Tuol Sleng interrogation centre in the city and killed by the Khmer Rouge. They were clubbed to death with sticks and farm implements, because bullets were too precious to waste. A *stupa*, or Buddhist shrine, containing the skulls of eight thousand of the victims and remnants of their clothing, bears witness not only to the brutality of the regime, but also to its leaders' acute distrust of everyone but themselves.

Distrust was at the heart of Khmer Rouge rule, and violence a product of it. Pol Pot mistrusted the outside world, so Cambodia's borders were sealed and neighbouring countries vilified; he mistrusted his own people, particularly those who were educated, so they were killed, or died of starvation and overwork; and he actively created distrust among the population by attempting to destroy human relationships. The result was a sinister climate of silence.

But as the suffering under the Khmer Rouge was ending, the hardship and the violence went on. Three hundred and sixty thousand Cambodians were beginning years of exile in crowded refugee camps in Thailand. Those who remained behind set to work to rebuild the obliterated foundations of their country, only to see a resumption of civil war. People began to forget what living in peace was like. The violence of the battlefield has spilled on to the streets of towns and villages. Scores are settled with AK-47s and grenades, rather than dialogue. People

Jim Holmes

◄ *The Buddhist shrine at Choeung Ek contains 8000 skulls of Khmer Rouge victims.*

use landmines to protect their property, rather than trust their neighbours. Domestic violence is widespread. Political killings are all too common and often go unpunished.

The consequence of the ever-turning cycle of violence has been the growing impoverishment of the Cambodian people. It follows, therefore, that only by breaking that cycle of violence and giving peace a chance can poverty be seriously addressed. And at last there is a chance for peace. Following the death of Pol Pot in mid-1998, the defection of Nuon Chea and Khieu Samphan, two of his senior henchmen, in early 1999, and the arrest of Ta Mok, 'the butcher', Pol Pot's former army chief, the Khmer Rouge are no longer a threat. For the first time in three decades, Cambodians have the oppor-tunity to make peace a reality for generations who have never known life without war.

▲ *Weapons are everywhere, and all too often are used in anger.*

Speaking with one voice

Peace may be a possibility, but lasting peace, built on the solid foundation of national reconciliation, will never be a reality until Cambodians trust one another again. Over the last decade they have been working together to rebuild trust and combat poverty. Sharing tasks and responsibilities within the community has had to be learned, however. Cambodians have traditionally looked no further than their own family unit for support. For that reason, one of the most hated aspects of life under the Khmer Rouge was communal living. The most obvious indication over the last ten years that people are coming together has been the establishment of hundreds of 'village development committees' (VDCs), whose main objective is to give people more control over their own lives. In the villages of Takorm, Toeun, and Krola, the VDCs have been effective in making real improvements to people's lives and in creating a feeling of solidarity among members. According to Tep Seng from Toeun: 'Without the committee, we would not have been in a position to take action against the loggers. The local authorities have not helped us, so it has been up to us to act – and we have done.' Similarly in Krola village the VDC has been instrumental in drawing up a request to the government to grant communal land rights to the village. Significantly, the committee is not seen as competing with the traditional tribal authority, but as supporting and advising it.

Chhoun Yeath believes the VDC to be a step forward for her village of Takorm: 'The rice bank has made villagers less dependent on the commercial rice-lenders and, consequently, less likely to get into debt, which can lead to people losing their land.' Just as important for Yeath is the way the members of the committee now work for each other and the rest of the village. 'Recently we became aware that a businessman was in the village, trying to buy up land. He had made some kind of deal with the district leader. We had a meeting and decided to go as a committee to speak to the businessman and the district leader. After we had talked to both, they agreed not to pursue the purchase of any land in the village. This was a great victory for us and proved that working together is effective.'

▲ *The Village Development Committee in Takorm village, one of hundreds established in Cambodia over the last ten years*

As the number of VDCs has grown, so there has been a rise in the number of local non-government organisations (NGOs), working *with*, rather than *on behalf of*, the poor to improve their lives. National NGOs were not permitted in Cambodia until 1991, though Oxfam and several other international agencies have been working there since 1979 with the full approval of the government. Now there are some 400 organisations, concerned with matters such as health care, education, agriculture, and human rights. They deserve credit for their role in supporting local initiatives to combat poverty and build community spirit. In Bondos Vichea in Phnom Penh, the Urban Sector Group (USG) has helped to establish a savings and credit scheme for residents, has facilitated work to improve drainage and reduce flooding in the area, and has recently organised pre-school classes. Sothea Phan of USG has noticed changes in the community. 'Before we began to help the community, the residents were not particularly interested in the quality of their lives. Conditions were very bad. They still are, but now people are making the effort to change their lives for the better, because they realise that they can make a difference if they work together. Before, they felt impotent. Now they are getting stronger. USG has simply been the catalyst for this important change of attitude. The challenge facing us all now is the threat of eviction by the government. But I am sure that the people living here will make their voices heard, because they know they are speaking together.'

No trust without justice

Youk Chhang shares Sothea Phan's opinion: 'Cambodians are learning to trust one another, because we know that we can't go back to the violence of the past. But I believe that trust can lead to genuine reconciliation only if those who have committed crimes against the Cambodian people are brought to justice.' Chhang is referring to crimes committed by the Khmer Rouge, for which no-one to date has been brought to trial. His own suffering is typical. He lost a sister and was separated from his mother for three years. Since then he has dedicated himself to the search for the truth, and is currently the director of the Documentation Centre of Cambodia and guardian of a 400,000-page archive, including Khmer Rouge government files, reports from prison guards, and signed confessions from the warders of Tuol Sleng interrogation centre. Chhang continues: 'The pain of Cambodians is still too great. It stops us remembering, but we cannot move forward until the past is confronted. Our aim is to provide objective information to enable people to deal with the past as they want to. It may be that individuals want to pursue cases against the Khmer Rouge, in which case we will support them.'

Chhang believes that ultimately justice can only be done by setting up an internationally recognised tribunal, probably under the auspices of the United Nations, to prosecute surviving members of the Khmer Rouge leadership, such as Ieng Sary (granted an amnesty by King Sihanouk), and Nuon Chea and Khieu Samphan, who recently surrendered to the authorities. 'This archive contains enough evidence to mount a trial,' says Chhang, 'but what is still missing is the political will of the Cambodian government, which may not want certain details from the past to emerge. Whatever happens, we will go on calling for a trial.'

▼ *Youk Chhang, archivist of the Khmer Rouge atrocities, consults his files*

Jim Holmes

Building trust, gaining strength, step by step

Thum Bunthan, of the Campaign to Reduce Violence for Peace in Battambang Province, sees continuing lack of trust as the main obstacle to lasting peace. 'Cambodians were betrayed by Pol Pot, who promised peace but brought only death. Successive governments have not won the trust of the people, because they are corrupt, and since we have had the so-called "free market", people have become more self-interested and less willing to help or trust one another.'

The peace movement was formed before the 1998 elections, when it became evident that the political campaigning risked inciting acts of violence and intimidation. A number of concerned individuals and organisations, both religious and secular, met in Phnom Penh and decided that ordinary Cambodians needed to be given the opportunity to express their opposition to political violence and demonstrate their desire for peace. Bunthan takes up the story: 'We organised a "March for Peace" in Battambang. We managed to persuade the provincial governor to grant us permission. On the day of the walk we met near the Sanghei Pagoda. One thousand Buddhist monks and two thousand ordinary citizens had gathered. Two days before, a grenade exploded near the pagoda, but that did not stop people attending. The marchers carried banners and slogans prepared by the school children of Battambang, and at least ten thousand spectators turned out to support us. Leaflets were handed out, explaining the reason for the walk. It was a great success, and I think the fact that there were so many people walking together with a common purpose gave them a feeling of strength.'

The march marked the beginning of a much wider campaign. Since the elections, much time and effort have gone into building a network of supporters who are interested in promoting peace through mutual trust and respect. What is especially interesting about the work of the campaign is the insistence that trust must not only be built at a grass-roots level, but must include influential Cambodians. 'We talk to national and local political leaders, members of the police and armed forces, judges and government officials, aiming to bring them into contact with religious bodies and ordinary citizens. By doing this, we create vertical alliances, making dialogue, trust, and understanding possible between different sections of society. Then, and only then, can we begin to get rid of the suspicion and work for a just society at peace with itself,' says Ok Kong, another peace campaigner.

Ok Kong and Thum Bunthan are both inspired and guided in their work by their faith in the Buddhist principles of tolerance and peace, and by the example of the Venerable Maha Ghosananda, a Cambodian cleric for whom peace is at the end of a long walk – a

▼ *Nearly 60,000 Buddhist monks died from starvation, disease, or execution during the Khmer Rouge years. Now monks are once again a focal point of village life, helping to restore a sense of trust among the people.*

Nic Dunlop

Dhammayietra. Since 1992 he has led annual peace marches throughout Cambodia, always accompanied by several thousand followers from all walks of life. In the past they have marched to call for a ban on landmines and an end to reckless deforestation. Along the way, the monks preach, and teach, the values of non-violence, wisdom, and compassion.

The long march to peace

Kim Leng is a non-violence trainer and member of the *Dhammayietra* preparation committee. She remembers the 1994 march as being especially significant for her and many others. 'We were walking to Pailin, which was occupied by the Khmer Rouge at the time. We were on Route 10 at the foot of the Chruy Snar mountain, walking in single file because many landmines had been laid by the roadside. Then we heard shooting and the sound of rockets. The monks at the front of the procession shouted back to be careful, but it was too late. Those at the front got caught in the crossfire. A monk and a nun were killed. Others were injured. We were all shocked and frightened by what had happened. We sat together to decide what to do next. Slowly, as we talked, people's fears left them. We began to feel strong and sure about what we were doing, so we decided to carry on towards Pailin. Local people came and joined us – many more than usual. The killing had not defeated us. It had made us all more determined to bring peace to our troubled country.'

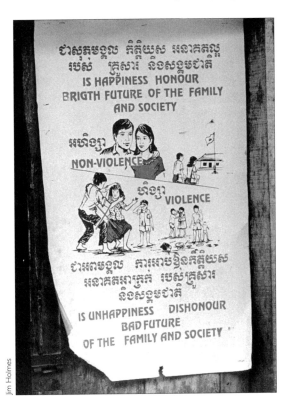

'Non-violence is happiness, honour, bright future of the family and society': a peace poster in Phnom Penh

Leng's words are echoed across Cambodia by a growing number of people who are taking steps to change Cambodia from a land of war to a place of peace, by rebuilding trust. Groups are forming everywhere, coming together with others to create alliances to press for change. In 1987 Maha Ghosananda led a contingent of Buddhist clerics to the UN-sponsored Cambodian peace talks in Jakarta, Indonesia. During the talks, he announced to the leaders of the four factions that he was founding a fifth army, 'an army of peace'. A reporter asked how effective such a force would be, and he replied: '[It will be] an army absolutely without guns or partisan politics, an army of reconciliation with so much courage that it turns away from violence, an army dedicated wholly to peace and to the end of suffering.' For ammunition, the army of peace would use 'bullets of loving kindness'.

The 'army of peace' is on the march, its numbers of 'soldiers' growing daily, their courage ever more resolute. The spirits of those who died at Choeung Ek and elsewhere are with them.

Elements of Cambodian culture

Jim Holmes

Buddhism today

Sok Hom is 29. He is in a dormitory, sitting beside his wooden bed. In the corner is a small desk, on which there is an English dictionary and an advanced maths book. Beside the books is an open packet of cigarettes and a Walkman stereo. Hom talks enthusiastically about studying foreign languages. He would like to travel when his studies are finished. Japan and the United States are first on the list. Above all, he dreams of becoming a film maker.

This is not a particularly startling encounter, except that Hom is a *Lok sang*: a Buddhist monk. Dressed in saffron robes draped over his bare shoulder, he is speaking from the Toul Tompong Pagoda in Phnom Penh, where he studies Pali, the language of religious texts, and Buddhist philosophy, as well as English and maths. If he fulfils his ambition of becoming a film maker, he will make films about religion. His first production will focus on the contrasts between traditional and modern aspects of Buddhism, and the definition of a new way forward for the priesthood, something in which he is particularly interested.

Sok Hom is not the only one debating these issues. Ever since activist monks took part in protest marches in Phnom Penh after the 1998 elections, the clergy and the general public have been asking whether monks should be involved in politics or should restrict themselves to routine religious matters, such as chanting, meditation, teaching, and collecting alms. Two monks allegedly died during the demonstrations, and many more were beaten up by the police in scenes that shocked Cambodians, who are always deeply respectful towards members of the clergy.

The controversy is nothing new for Buddhist monks in Cambodia, who belong to the branch known as *Theravada* ('Way of the Elders').

▲ *Burning incense at the pagoda of Wat Phnom: Buddhism is enjoying a revival in Cambodia, following its suppression by the Pol Pot regime.*

Buddhism came to Cambodia from northern India via Sri Lanka, Burma, and Thailand in the fifth century AD, gradually replacing the Hindu cults of Shiva and Vishnu. It became the state religion of Cambodia some 800 years later, during the Angkor period. Since the thirteenth century the only threat to the survival of Buddhism has come from the Khmer Rouge in the 1970s, who almost succeeded in destroying it. Of 62,000 monks, barely 3000 survived. Some of the 3600 temples were damaged or destroyed. Now numbers of monks are back to pre-1975 levels, and temples are being built in every town and village, in recognition of the importance of Buddhism to the lives of ordinary people. Ninety-five per cent of the population, mainly Khmer and Chinese, are Buddhist.

While preaching the Buddha's message of tolerance, peace, and faith, Cambodian monks have been walking a tightrope between peace and politics for the last 150 years. During the struggle for independence from French rule, monks played leading roles. Anti-French clerics organised an army of 5000 peasants in the 1860s. It was quickly put down, but efforts by monks to regain Cambodia's freedom continued. In the 1940s, Achar Hem Chieu protested against French plans to romanise the Khmer script (as had been done in Vietnam). In 1942, he was arrested for preaching anti-French sermons to Khmer troops. His arrest sparked off a protest march which saw police and monks use violence against each other.

People today are drawing parallels between the activities of Achar Hem Chieu and the monks who took part in the recent demonstrations, which ended in violence. While condemning the behaviour of the riot police, many Cambodians, however, remain uneasy at the prospect of Buddhist monks openly acting in the political arena. They cite the example of the Venerable Maha Ghosananda, who has always kept away from mainstream politics and, consequently, has always been able to maintain a neutral stance, earning him the trust and respect of all, and enabling him to play important mediation roles, as he did in 1987 and 1988 during negotiations among the various Cambodian political factions.

Activist monks think otherwise. Their argument is that monks have been allowed to vote in elections since 1993 and are therefore obliged to take an active, but non-violent role in politics. And they highlight the fact that Cambodian Buddhism already has a highly politicised clergy, with the heads of different sects sympathetic to different political parties.

And so the debate goes on ...

Keeping traditions alive: celebrating the Water Festival

Bun Sophea is a farmer from Kandal, facing the prospects of yet another poor harvest. But while he is in Phnom Penh, he can temporarily forget his problems. Here he is an oarsman, proud member of a 60-man team, racing through the foaming, chocolate-brown waters of the Tonle Sap in 'Mohamia' (Big Dragon), a red- and green-striped longboat, pitting skill and strength against other competitors for honour and glory. There is no outright winner, but the best crews receive awards from the King.

This is the annual water festival, *Bon Om Touk*, held over three days

▼ *Longboats prepare to race on the Tonle Sap river during the annual water festival in Phnom Penh*

Jim Holmes

in early November to mark the end of the rainy season and the full moon of the Buddhist month of *Kadeuk*. It is the most popular of all Cambodia's national celebrations. Three hundred boats, with one thousand crew members, men and women, race in pairs over a 1700m stretch of the river, finishing in front of the royal palace, just north of the confluence of the Tonle Sap and Mekong rivers. Their families, along with thousands of spectators, jostle for space on the embankment to catch a glimpse of their favourite boats. Street vendors, selling everything from plastic day-glo windmills to creamy white turtle eggs, help to make the festival a colourful spectacle.

'The water festival is an important part of Khmer culture,' explains Sophea, as he dons the team's colours before the next race. 'We are celebrating a great naval victory against foreign invaders and, at the same time, we give thanks for the flooding of the river, which brings us rice and fish.' Historians trace the origins of the festival back to the reign of Jayavarman II in the twelfth century, when a naval victory against Burma brought peace to the ancient world. Legend has it that the jubilant monarch sent his fleet of ships to the place where the Mekong and Tonle Sap rivers converge. In this show of military might, the ships churned up the waters into a whirlpool so powerful that the flow of the Tonle Sap River was reversed, bringing down fish and nutrient-rich water from the Great Lake to feed the people and nourish the land. Later naval victories against the Cham in the thirteenth century and the Siamese in the sixteenth established the festival firmly in popular culture.

Like many celebrations, the water festival is infused with both secular tradition and religious symbolism. At the end of the races, around 5 o'clock in the afternoon, Sophea and the rest of the team will go to a nearby Buddhist temple. 'We will burn incense, pray, and give presents of rice and fruit to the monks, while we wait for the *Kadeuk* moon. If the moon shines brightly, this is a sign that the harvest will be good and that there will be peace,' says Sophea.

Does he think the moon will be bright this time? 'I'm not sure,' he says, smiling wryly. 'Cambodia certainly needs peace. Maybe an ancient king will come back and restore peace to our country. Maybe things will be OK. I don't want to think too much about it now. I'm here to enjoy myself while I can. Back in Kandal, there hasn't been enough rain. My rice crop won't be good. I may lose my land. Things are probably going to get worse before they get better.'

Mike Goldwater

Cambodian dance: bringing history and culture to life

Their movements are slow, fluid, measured. Head still, forearms tilted upwards, supple wrists twisting gently, outstretched fingers arching backwards, then gliding into different poses, caressing the air. The feet are bare, turned outwards, the legs bent slightly at the knees, cushioning the gestures of the upper body. They move in unison, dressed in brightly

coloured leotards and leggings. Some smile as they dance. Others are concentrating too hard to smile.

The young girls are performing a routine from the *Reamker*, an adaptation of the Indian Hindu epic, the *Ramayana*, introduced into Cambodian culture 2000 years ago. The dance is widely performed throughout Cambodia, where the Indian original has been fused with colourful Khmer myth and folklore. At the heart of the story is the triumph of good over evil, love over hatred, as Ream, the god-hero, defeats Ravana, the brutal king who has kidnapped Sita, Ream's wife. Ream and Sita are finally reconciled with the help of the gods. It has everything an epic needs: raucous battles, tender love scenes, and the exotic appearance of Hanuman, the magical monkey-general and his army.

This is no ordinary dance troupe, however. The girls are practising in the back yard of a house in the suburbs of Phnom Penh under the watchful eye of Vung Metrey, a former dancer with the renowned National Dance Company. Metrey has only just established her Apsara Arts Association, after finally getting permission from the local authorities, but the wait has been worth it. 'I was desperate to give poor girls and boys in this area the opportunity to become a part of Cambodian culture. Dance brings history and culture to life. It shows the importance of Cambodian women, that they are the soul of the nation. And dance is a way of showing that we

▲ Girls from the Apsara Arts Association performing the Reamker, the Cambodian national dance

have survived the past and can look forward to the future.'

The association has yet to present its first public performance, but Metrey has already chosen the dance. It is not the *Reamker*, but a previously forgotten work called *Ketanak Pon* ('national pride'), which she has revived. Set in ancient times, before the rise of the Angkor empire, the dance tells the story of a country embroiled in bitter civil war, where families are separated, and left to agonise about the fate of loved ones. Weakened by internal conflict, the country falls prey to attack from outside.

Metrey explains the reason for her choice. 'The *Ketanak Pon* dance gives a clear message: Cambodians must unite and work together. Only then can we be strong enough to defeat a common enemy. I'm not talking about the Khmer Rouge. I'm talking about poverty. That is Cambodia's biggest enemy, and unless we take steps now, our nation will always be divided. Here our weapon against poverty is dance, and we will use it.'

Cambodia at the crossroads

A people's vote for peace

'July 26 1998 was an important day for me,' says Chhoun Yeath. 'I voted for peace and a better future for me and my children. Now it's up to the politicians to work together and to make sure that the peace holds.'

Jim Holmes

▲ *Will the chasm between rich and poor in Cambodia grow even wider and deeper?*

Yeath was among the 90 per cent of Cambodians who cast their vote. It was an impressive turnout, despite pre-election violence, according to the United Nations and local human-rights organisations, including ADHOC. 'The elections were not perfect,' admits Thun Saray, the President of ADHOC, 'but we can accept them, because election day was peaceful, and vote counting was conducted reasonably fairly.' The international community passed the same verdict.

Hun Sen's Cambodian People's Party (CPP) topped the polls, gaining the most seats in parliament, but falling short of the two-thirds majority needed to form a government. Five months of political wrangling followed, until a deal was struck and endorsed by King Sihanouk: Hun Sen became Prime Minister, while his rival, Prince Norodom Ranariddh of FUNCINPEC, was appointed Speaker of the Parliament. This is potentially a positive change. Gone is the power-sharing arrangement that so paralysed the last government. The CPP has almost a free hand to govern as it thinks fit, and in a country where, after the demise of the Khmer Rouge, the prospects for a durable peace have not been better since Independence in 1953.

Hun Sen knows that Cambodia stands at a crossroads and that his government can either exploit the peace dividend for the good of the vast majority of Cambodians, or it can stand by and watch the chasm between rich and poor grow wider and deeper. But poverty cannot be tackled unless the government has the political will and the courage to carry out meaningful reforms. There must be firm resolve to rein in the corrupt politicians, judges, police, and army officers, and to confront the businesspeople who buy their favours as a means to get rich quick, rather than investing in long-term projects, creating jobs and other benefits for the economy. And the government must be seen to address Cambodia's long-standing social problems by improving services such as health care and education, and by guaranteeing ordinary citizens their fundamental human rights. The overriding task is thus to restore Cambodians' trust in those who govern, by establishing the rule of law.

If, on the other hand, the poverty gap does not narrow, there is sure to be resentment on the part of those denied the chance of a decent livelihood – resentment which the Khmer Rouge skilfully exploited to build their power-base in the late 1960s and early 1970s before their decisive victory in 1975. No Cambodian wants to see a return to Year Zero.

A turn for the better?

Since taking office, Hun Sen has used his 'honeymoon' period to announce changes in government policies and priorities. Acknowledging the end of the civil war, he has promised to reduce spending on the army and police force by cutting numbers by over 50 per cent to 80,000 – on condition that the international donor community provides £100 million in redundancy payments. Money saved on defence spending, according to the Prime Minister, will be used to improve 'social affairs and public health'. This is potentially good news for Cambodia's poor, especially the rural poor, who lack decent clinics, hospitals, schools, clean water, and proper sanitation. The government has also pledged to crack down on illegal logging, though not for the first time.

If the government is sincere in its intentions, the international community may be prepared to support its efforts through increased aid to health and education projects, to help to settle displaced people, and to de-mine land for housing and agriculture. Now that security has improved throughout the country, the government must make sure that resources are targeted on areas of genuine need. Currently, most aid money goes to projects in Phnom Penh, even though the vast majority of the poor live outside the capital. If the urban–rural poverty divide is to be narrowed, resources must be more equally distributed, and more use made of efficient local organisations, rather than sometimes overpriced foreign agencies.

Peace: a boost to the economy?

July 1997 was the month when Cambodia was due to become the tenth member of the Association of South East Asian Nations (ASEAN), a vast free-trade zone of 500 million potential customers. It was not to be. Fighting between factions of the army loyal to CPP

Jim Holmes

and FUNCINPEC, which resulted in Hun Sen seizing power from Prince Ranariddh, with whom he had shared it, led to ASEAN taking the unprecedented decision to refuse entry to Cambodia until political stability was restored. Some eight months after the elections, on 30 April 1999, Cambodia was finally admitted to the association, whose members, until recently, boasted some of the fastest rates of economic growth in the world.

Growth turned to recession among the ASEAN members in 1998, although their economies now seem to be recovering. Thailand, Cambodia's neighbour, has been harder hit than most, and this has affected the Cambodian economy as well. Indonesia and Malaysia are facing additional political upheaval in the wake of the economic slump. Cambodia certainly did not join at a propitious moment, but commentators agree that its relatively low labour costs and favourable tax breaks for businesses should attract external investment and thus create employment in the medium term. The downside is the membership fee of US$5 million, the cost to the state for officials to attend nearly 300 ASEAN meetings a year, and the gradual reduction of tariffs on trade which will constitute a significant loss of revenue to the Treasury and may increase unemployment and threaten the market-share of some local enterprises.

Peace should also attract much-needed revenue from tourists, eager to explore the ancient temples of Angkor, soak up the sun on the white beaches of Kompong Som, or trek through the upland forests of Ratanakiri. Tourism is potentially a major source of hard currency for the government and private sector, yet to be fully tapped because of insecurity.

▼ *Cambodia dot.com: an advertisement for Microsoft products in a Phnom Penh street*

Jim Holmes

Or a turn for the worse?

Hun Sen has been saying the right things since his re-election, garnering popular support and pleasing the international aid donors, but how committed is his administration to carrying out the reforms that will bring tangible benefits to ordinary Cambodians? And even if the government is committed, does it have the political power to carry them out? Contrary to statistics which show a slight decrease in poverty levels from 39 per cent in 1993 to 36 per cent in 1998, our families report that it is becoming more difficult for them to make a decent enough living to provide adequate food, shelter, medicine, and schooling. The main reason for this in rural areas is that people are finding it increasingly difficult to get access to good arable land, forest, and fishing grounds, on which they depend for their livelihoods. And as people in the countryside slide further into poverty, they migrate to the towns in the hope of finding decent jobs – as Vanna, Savou, and Samon did. They are invariably disappointed. Their needs for jobs, housing, health care, and education can no longer be met in the urban areas. The result is growing poverty and despair in places like Bondos Vichea, where the residents are now facing eviction.

The key to Cambodia's recovery lies in its natural resources – but it may be too late to stop their destruction. At current rates of exploitation, Cambodia's forests will be commercially logged out in three to five years, according to the World Bank; fish stocks could fall to irrecoverable levels; rivers will silt up; droughts will ruin harvests. An environmental catastrophe is becoming a probability, rather than a possibility. The livelihoods of millions of Cambodians are hanging in the balance. The government's only hope is to crack down on those who are taking too much and giving back nothing. There have been successful raids on several illegal sawmills, but the government's commitment to the long-term protection of the forests will always be questionable as long as Hun Sen remains personally implicated in illegal logging (according to Global Witness, which monitors the destruction of Cambodia's forests). The international community is concerned by what is happening, but is unlikely to be unduly worried, because Cambodia is no longer a country of any strategic value.

The situation, however, is not hopeless. Cambodians chose the CPP to run the country, and they therefore have the right to demand that the government fulfils its election promises and puts Cambodia's house in order.

Jim Holmes

▲ *Is it too late to stop the destruction of Cambodia's precious natural resources?*

People power making a difference

In the past, autocratic leaders of Cambodia have never taken much notice of the wishes of ordinary Cambodian citizens. Nor have Cambodians had the opportunity to make their voice heard. Democratic principles do not run deep here, or anywhere else in south-east Asia. But this is changing: President Suharto of Indonesia, one of the last 'dinosaurs' of the region, has been swept away, and Mahatir Mohammed, Prime Minister of Malaysia, is under pressure to make political reforms. The people of Cambodia, too, are eager for change. Despite an almost instinctive cautiousness, born of a legacy of irresponsible and cruel leadership, and a distrust of politicians, Cambodians sense that they have an historic

Jim Holmes

opportunity to break with their violent past and look forward to a brighter, more peaceful future. Several years ago, Yeath had very few expectations for her children. Now she wants her young son and daughter to go on to further education and train as teachers or doctors. She insists that she will not hold her daughter back. Samon wants a secure future for her children – possibly full-time jobs at the local factory. Vanna would like her children to find permanent work and decent accommodation, preferably not in Phnom Penh.

People sense the authority that has been vested in the government at the recent elections, and there is a growing determination to make sure that their leaders act responsibly. Ordinary people no longer feel powerless. They have a voice through their VDCs, NGOs, and Buddhist organisations, which together constitute a maturing civil society, an 'army for peace'. People are beginning to lose their fear of criticising government – a fact for which the government is also to be commended. After the elections there were street demonstrations, organised by the opposition, to protest against voting irregularities and to call for peace. People made their dissatisfaction known, because they realised they no longer stood alone. They realise that they can make a difference if they stand together. They understand this because they are learning to trust each other again. Cambodian leaders must work hard to deliver on promises and gain the people's trust. That will take time.

Cambodians are willing to wait. They understand the complexities of rebuilding a fractured, traumatised society with limited financial and human resources. They are aware that improvements to health services and education cannot be delivered overnight, and they recognise the government's efforts to bring about peace. Cambodians will wait, but maybe a little less patiently than before.

Facts and figures

Population
11,430,000 (based on 1998 census);
52 per cent female, 48 per cent male;
16 per cent urban, 84 per cent rural

Annual population growth
2.4 per cent

Languages
Khmer (official); minority languages

Religion
Theravada Buddhism (95 per cent)

Land area
181,035 sq km

Life expectancy (at birth)
54 years

Maternal mortality rate
900 deaths per 100,000 live births (UK:11)

Infant (under one year) mortality rate
110 deaths per 1,000 live births (UK:7)

Under-five mortality rate
174 deaths per 1,000 live births (UK:9)

Proportion of the population below the poverty line[1]
36 per cent

Access to health services
urban 80 per cent,
rural 50 per cent

Access to safe drinking water
urban 61 per cent,
rural 28 per cent

Access to safe sanitation
urban 71 per cent,
rural 6 per cent

Jim Holmes

Enrolment in lower-secondary education
urban male 57 per cent,
rural female 12 per cent

Literacy rates[2]
urban male adult 87 per cent,
rural female adult 52 per cent

Gross domestic product per capita
$286

Government budget (1998)
$420 million

Currency
Riel (6,000 Riel = approximately £1 – April 1999)

Estimated inflation rate (1998)
20 per cent

Annual growth rate (1998)
3.5 per cent

Main economic activities
rice (14 per cent of GDP),
other crops and rubber (10 per cent),
livestock (13 per cent),
manufacturing (8 per cent),
fisheries (3.5 per cent),
forest products (3 per cent)

Value of exports (1996)
$659 million – sawn timber ($96m);
logs ($53m); rubber ($32m)

Sources

- 'Women's Contribution to Development', Cambodia Human Development Report 1998 (Cambodian Ministry of Planning/ United Nations Development Programme, 1998)
- General Population Census of Cambodia (Ministry of Planning, 1998)
- 'Towards a Better Future: An Analysis of the Situation of Children and Women in Cambodia' (UNICEF, 1996)
- Monthly Bulletin of Statistics (Ministry of Economy and Finance, July 1998)
- 'Cambodia: Progress in Recovery and Reform' (The World Bank, 1997)
- *Going Places: Cambodia's Future on the Move* (Global Witness, 1998)

Notes

1 The poverty line is defined as an income of approximately 1500 Riels per capita per day, which equals approximately 50 pence at 1997 rates for the Riel.
2 According to the United Nations Development Programme report of 1997, the overall literacy rate is estimated at 35 per cent, based on the Human Development Index for Cambodia.
3 According to Global Witness, illegal exports from January 1997 to end February 1998 totalled $577 million.

Dates and events

3rd century AD Founding of coastal state of Funan.

6th century Funan incorporated into inland state of Chenla.

802 Jayavarman II (802–850) founds the Angkor Kingdom, north of the Tonle Sap.

12th century Construction of Angkor Wat temple by Suryavarman II (1113-1150).

1177 Cham pillage and burn the wooden capital city of Angkor to the ground.

c1200 Jayavarman VII (1181–1219) rebuilds the capital in the same place as before and also rebuilds the royal city, Angkor Thom.

1431 Siam (now Thailand) invades and occupies the city of Angkor. The golden age of the Angkor empire draws to a close.

Late 18th century Cambodia loses permanent control over the Mekong Delta to the Vietnamese.

1840s Siamese and Vietnamese armies fight on Cambodian territory, devastating the country.

1864 Cambodia becomes a French protectorate.

1884 Cambodia becomes a French colony, along with Laos and Vietnam in the Union Indochinoise.

Jim Holmes

1953 Cambodia gains independence from France.

1965 Having backed North Vietnam, Prince Sihanouk's government severs links with the United States following deployment of US troops in Vietnam.

1970 Lon Nol topples Sihanouk in a *coup d'état*. He becomes the first President of the Khmer Republic.

1975 Khmer Rouge under Pol Pot seize power. The country is renamed Democratic Kampuchea.

1979 Vietnam invades, following Khmer Rouge attacks, ousts the Pol Pot regime and establishes a pro-Vietnamese Cambodian government.

1981 The country is renamed the People's Republic of Kampuchea.

1982 Coalition government-in-exile formed in Thailand comprising the Sihanoukists, Khmer Rouge, and the anti-Communist Khmer People's National Liberation Front (KPNLF). Despite evidence of genocide, the coalition is recognised by the United Nations as the legitimate government of Cambodia and retains the seat at the UN. This is due to pressure from China and the USA. both virulently anti-Vietnamese.

1989 Country renamed State of Cambodia as the last Vietnamese troops prepare to leave, following international agreement.

1991 The Paris Peace Agreement is signed.

1993 Elections held under the supervision of the United Nations Transitional Authority in Cambodia (UNTAC). Country becomes a constitutional monarchy with Norodom Sihanouk as King.

1997 Fighting erupts in Phnom Penh and elsewhere between factions of the army loyal to second Prime Minister, Hun Sen, and first Prime Minister, Prince Norodom Ranariddh. Ranariddh flees to France. Hun Sen carries out a crackdown on Ranariddh supporters. A number of deaths reported. Hun Sen consolidates his power.

1998 Pol Pot dies in the Khmer Rouge stronghold of Anlong Veng, following factional split in the leadership. Defection of most remaining Khmer Rouge troops to the government.

1998 National elections. Hun Sen becomes sole Prime Minister. Ranariddh takes the post of Speaker of the National Assembly.

1999 Defection of last two survivors of the Khmer Rouge leadership, Khieu Samphan and Nuon Chea, and alleged capture of Ta Mok, Pol Pot's army chief.

Sources and further reading

Chanda, N. (1986), *Brother Enemy: the War after the War*, New York: Macmillan

Chandler, D.P. (1991), *The Tragedy of Cambodian History: Politics, War and Revolution since 1945*, New Haven: Yale University Press

Chandler, D.P. (1992), *Brother Number One: A Political Biography of Pol Pot*, Colorado: Westview Press

Chandler, D.P. (1993), *A History of Cambodia*, Colorado: Westview Press

Drabble, M. (1992), *The Gates of Ivory*, London: Penguin

Kiernan, B. (1985), *How Pol Pot Came to Power*, London: Verso

Kiernan, B. (1996), *The Pol Pot Regime: Race, Power, and Genocide in Cambodia under the Khmer Rouge, 1975–79*, New Haven: Yale University Press

May, S. (1986), *Cambodian Witness*, London: Faber and Faber

Mouhot, H. (1986), *Travels in Indochina*, Bangkok: White Lotus

Mysliwiec, E. (1988), *Punishing the Poor: the International Isolation of Kampuchea*, Oxford: Oxfam

Ponchaud, F. (1978), *Cambodia after Year Zero* (translated from French), London: Penguin

Shawcross, W. (1979; revised 1986), *Sideshow: Kissinger, Nixon and the Destruction of Cambodia*, London: Chatto and Windus

Shawcross, W, (1984), *The Quality of Mercy: Cambodia, Holocaust and the Modern Conscience*, London: Fontana.

Swain, J. (1985), *River of Time*, London: Minerva

Vickery, M. (1984), *Cambodia 1975–1982*, London: Allen and Unwin

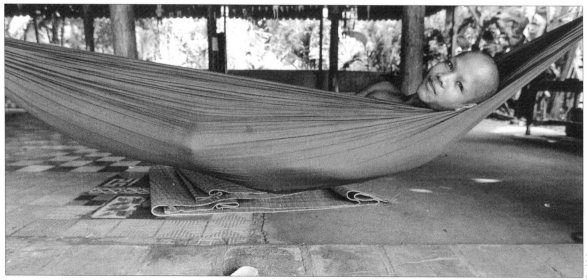

Jim Holmes

Acknowledgements

This book would never have been written without the help of all the Cambodian people whose stories I have tried to tell. The trust they showed in me, their openness, honesty, and hospitality taught me much. To Biranchi Upadhyaya and his team in the Oxfam GB office in Phnom Penh, especially Rithi, my faithful interpreter, go my heartfelt thanks. I also thank Jim Holmes, the photographer, for his outstanding professionalism and commitment to the project. Paul Valentin, Siddo Deva, Shiva Kumar, Michael Hayes, and Eva Mysliwiec offered support as well as constructive criticism. And last, but not least, thanks to Catherine Robinson of Oxfam Publishing, who gave me the opportunity to write the book and whose faith in me gave me strength.

Ian Brown

▶ *Din Sophia in Sak Phoy village, Battambang, feeds a pig bought with a loan from a local community-development group.*

Nic Dunlop

Oxfam in Cambodia

Most of the communities and projects featured in this book are supported by Oxfam GB. Oxfam's relationship with Cambodia began in August 1979, with a delivery of food and medicine to a country laid waste by the Khmer Rouge revolution. An Oxfam office was opened in Phnom Penh in 1981, and supplies of emergency aid gradually gave way to a programme of infrastructural rehabilitation, together with lobbying and advocacy to end the international isolation of Cambodia.

In 1992 the focus of Oxfam's work in Cambodia changed from technical assistance and support for government institutions to developing the capacity of local non-government organisations serving the needs of poor and marginalised communities. More than 25 partner groups are currently supported. They work on a range of programmes, including micro-credit schemes, community-based natural resource management, food security, research and advocacy on land-rights issues, support for civil and political rights, conflict resolution, campaigning against domestic violence, and support for basic education and primary health care services.

▲ A villager in Takorm tends his cow, supplied by a livestock bank run by Oxfam's local partner, Aphivat Strey

Cambodia has made great progress since 1979 in restoring civil society and building up the infrastructure necessary for self-sufficiency. But there is still much work to be done. Cambodia remains one of the poorest nations in Asia, and within the country there are great social inequalities. Alongside six other members of Oxfam International (Oxfam America, Oxfam Hong Kong, Community Aid Abroad, Novib, Oxfam Solidarité (Belgium), and Oxfam Quebec), Oxfam GB will continue to work on community development with its partners in Cambodia, promoting and supporting the rights of all members of society to a secure and sustainable livelihood, good education and health care, freedom from violence, full civil and political rights, and equality between men and women. Oxfam believes that the poverty of individuals, communities, and whole nations is not inevitable, and must be ended.

Index